Typewriting Theory and Practice

Also Published by Chambers

Leafe: PRACTICAL TYPING SKILLS
Wareing: PROGRESSIVE AUDIO-TYPING

Typewriting Theory and Practice

Joyce Stananought, BEd(Hons), FRSA, has many years' experience of teaching secretarial skills, word processing and computer applications in both further education colleges and secondary schools. She was formerly Principal Lecturer and Deputy Head of Department of Business Information Processing at Salford College of Technology.

Joyce has been involved as an examiner for typewriting and other secretarial subjects for several years and this experience has helped her to develop a simple, practical and straightforward approach in the preparation of instructional material for students at all levels.

She is well-known as a writer and lecturer both in this country and overseas and has more recently become involved with the production of teaching aids and learning materials concerned with information processing.

TYPEWRITING THEORY AND PRACTICE

ASSIGNMENT BOOK

Joyce Stananought, BEd(Hons), FRSA

Chambers

Published by W & R Chambers Ltd, Edinburgh 1987

British Library Cataloguing in Publication Data

Stananought, Joyce
    Typewriting: theory and practice:
    assignment book.
    1. Typewriting—Examinations, questions, etc.
    I. Title
    652.2'0076   Z49.2
ISBN 0 550 75304 4

Set by Blackwood Pillans & Wilson, Ltd. Edinburgh

Printed in Great Britain at the University Press, Cambridge

CONTENTS

This book contains a wide range of assignments related to *Typewriting Theory and Practice—A Progressive Course*. The assignments within each section concentrate on the typewriting skills listed below.

CHECKLIST AND PROGRESS CHART

Use this checklist to record your progress.

Record the time it takes you to type and check each assignment.

Section number	Theory points covered	Assignment number	Date completed	Time taken
1	Basic rules of typewriting display	Test questions 1–11		
2	Spacing after punctuation	1	_____	_____
	Open punctuation style	2	_____	_____
	Courtesy titles	3	_____	_____
	Initials and qualifications	4	_____	_____
	Names and addresses for mailing	5	_____	_____
		6	_____	_____
3	Main headings and sub-headings	7	_____	_____
	Shoulder headings	8	_____	_____
	Paragraph headings	9	_____	_____
	Marginal headings (side headings)	10	_____	_____
	Inset items (indented items)	11	_____	_____
	Indented and hanging paragraph style	12	_____	_____
4	Placement of text on the page	13	_____	_____
	(vertical centring)	14	_____	_____
	Typing from manuscript	15	_____	_____
	Manuscript correction signs	16	_____	_____
	Abbreviations	17	_____	_____
	Reference symbols and footnotes			
	Leaving space of specified size			
5	Centred layout—horizontal	18	_____	_____
	centring	19	_____	_____
	Centring over the page	20	_____	_____
	Centring over the typing line	21	_____	_____
	Block centring	22	_____	_____
	Justified right margin of displayed work	23	_____	_____
	Justified right margin of text			

Section number	Theory points covered	Assignment number	Date completed	Time taken
6	Memos	24		
	Memos on memo-headed paper	25		
	Memos on plain paper	26		
	Continuation sheets for memos	27		
		28		
		29		
		30		
7	File copies	31		
	Carbon copies	32		
	Distribution copies	33		
	Bring forward notes on file copies	34		
		35		
		36		
8	Lists of items	37		
	Numbered and lettered paragraphs	38		
	Metric and imperial units of	39		
	measurement	40		
	Mathematical signs and symbols	41		
	Symbols for British and foreign	42		
	currency	43		
	Use of words and figures	44		
9	Typing simple forms	45		
	Completion of forms	46		
	Typing on card	47		
		48		
		49		
		50		
		51		
		52		
		53		
		54		

Section number	Theory points covered	Assignment number	Date completed	Time taken
10	Leader dots	55		
	Ditto	56		
	Ellipsis	57		
	Accents	58		
	Square brackets	59		
	The brace	60		
		61		
		62		
		63		
11	Business letters	64		
	Stationery	65		
	Information always included on a business letter	66 67		
	Details which may be included on a business letter	68 69		
	Standard circular letter	70		
	Form letters with 'personalised' variable details	71 72		
	Continuation sheets for business letters	73		
	Semi-blocked layout			
	Personal letters			
	Business postcards			
12	Typing numbers and totals in columns	74		
	Column layout	75		
	Tables with column headings	76		
	Tables incorporated into other documents	77		
	Tables with horizontal ruling	78		
	Tables with horizontal and vertical ruling	79		
	Tables with divided columns	80		
	Leader dots to tables	81		
	Reference signs and footnotes to tables	82		

INTRODUCTION

Typewriting Theory and Practice—Assignment Book provides a progressively graded programme of assignments to test your knowledge of typewriting theory and your typewriting or word processing skills.

The book contains a wide range of assignments, grouped into 12 major theory sections. Each section includes assignments involving a variety of the skills required in today's office:

    typing from manuscript

    typing from corrected typescript

    proof-reading

    short-answer theory tests

    correction of deliberate errors in spelling, punctuation, use of apostrophe, grammar or
      consistency

The assignments test typewriting and word processing skills over a wide range of theory from elementary to intermediate level. These theory points are fully explained in *Typewriting Theory and Practice—A Progressive Course* by the same author.

You may wish to use the two books as companion texts, using the *Assignment Book* material as revisionary tests at the end of each section of *A Progressive Course*, or when you have worked your way completely through *A Progressive Course*.

However, each book stands on its own, and the Assignment Book provides a useful revision and test book for all typists, from elementary to advanced level.

ASSIGNMENTS

Before you start to type an assignment, ensure that you have all the stationery you need, together with your pencil, pen, ruler and correction material. Select the appropriate size of paper, and set the line spacing, margins, tabular stops, etc.

Read through the assignment, using your dictionary to check on spellings where necessary. Take care to follow any special instructions accurately.

DECISION-MAKING

Instructions on paper sizes, margins, line spacing, etc, to be used for the assignments, are kept to a minimum. You are expected to make your own decisions in these areas, unless specific instructions are given. By experimenting with various styles of layout you can build up experience and judgement on the most effective forms of display.

HEADED PAPER

Samples of letter-headed paper and memo-headed paper are provided on pages 107 and 108. You may photocopy these headed papers for use in typing the assignments in this book, so that you gain realistic practice in presenting work in the form required in an office.

KEYS TO ASSIGNMENTS

Worked examples of the assignments are provided on pages 51 to 104 so that you can compare your work with suggested layouts. Remember that these are only *examples* of the way in which each assignment may be laid out. You may have decided to use different margins or line spacing, but your layout will be just as acceptable as long as you have correctly applied points of theory to your practical work. The most important factor is that your completed work should be accurate and that any corrections are unobtrusively made.

IF YOU USE A WORD PROCESSOR

The assignments in this book are based on business material and provide a sound preparation for office typewriting. The approach and the styles presented take into account the impact word processing is having on typewriting skills for business. The book will therefore prove useful if you are learning to use a word processor.

1 BASIC RULES OF TYPEWRITING DISPLAY

TEST QUESTIONS

Test your knowledge of basic typewriting display by answering the following questions before starting to work through the assignments.

(1) Type size is measured in 'characters per inch'. The 2 main sizes of type in general use are:

Pica type, which has . . . characters to 1″, also known as . . . Pitch.
Elite type, which has . . . characters to 1″, also known as . . . Pitch.

(2) There are . . . lines of type to 1″.

(3) Minimum sizes for margins on most documents should be:

Left . . .
Right . . .
Top . . .
Bottom . . .

(4) Which of the following words should not be divided at the end of a line? Where would you divide the remaining words?

once-over	print-out	consumables
19,724-37,605	paragraphs	OXFAM
circumspect	processing	Mr G W K Wynn-Chase
1998-1999	throughout	straight
through	workforce	comprehensive

(5) What style of paragraph layout and what line spacing have been used for the following paragraphs of text?

```
Private Company Health-Care Plan are currently providing
    employee cover for thousands of employees in large,
    medium and small companies.

The many benefits include hospital accommodation and
    treatment, specialists' fees and a wide range of other
    medical charges - up to £45,000 per year for each
    employee.
```

(6) What style of paragraph layout and what line spacing have been used for the paragraphs of text below?

```
Our internal mail distribution trolley has shielded wheels

to avoid damage to desks and doorways - and possible

injury to members of staff.  Two steel wire mesh plastic

coated removable baskets are fitted to the trolley.


The trolley is highly manoeuvrable over all surfaces.  It

is light enough to move easily, yet strong enough for the

busiest mailroom.
```

(7) What style of paragraph layout and what line spacing have been used for the paragraphs of text below?

> Today's sophisticated new office blocks need complex
>
> services if they are to function efficiently and provide a
>
> pleasant working environment for members of staff.
>
> Specialist companies offer expertise in designing,
>
> fabricating and installing vital services such as heating,
>
> ventilation, air conditioning, plumbing, electrical power,
>
> lighting, fire protection and communication systems.

(8) Give the measurements of the following paper sizes in millimetres:
A4, A5, A6.

(9) How many sheets are there in a ream of paper?

(10) State the number of character spaces (Elite and Pica) across the page for the following paper sizes: A4 portrait; A5 portrait; A5 landscape.

(11) State the number of line spaces available down the page for the following paper sizes: A4 portrait; A5 portrait; A5 landscape.

If you use a printer fitted with computer listing paper, find the width of your paper in millimetres and in character spaces, and the depth of the paper in line spaces. You will need this information to help you display your work when you start the assignments in the following sections.

2 PUNCTUATION, COURTESY TITLES, NAMES AND ADDRESSES FOR MAILING

Assignment 1

Type in blocked paragraph style in double line spacing. Use wide margins. Type abbreviations as shown.

Are there times when you would like to hire a video film but are put off by the thought of having to travel to your local video club — and of having to travel there again to return the film? Here's your answer! The "TWO-SOME VIDEO CLUB" will call at your home twice a week — on Tuesdays and Fridays between 6.00 pm and 10.00 pm with a travelling video library.

If you haven't got a video recorder, you can hire one from our parent company — "TIMES-TWO TV" — at very competitive rates. We shall be calling on you this week to introduce our new mobile video service.

Assignment 2

Type in blocked paragraph style in 1½ line spacing. Use wide margins. Type abbreviations as shown.

Fiona McGovern is a young golfer seeking sponsorship so that she can take part in the European Ladies' Golf Tour next year. Many of her friends and colleagues feel that Miss McGovern has a good future in world class golf — but she has a problem! She is stuck in her home country of New Zealand, unable to afford the fare to the UK and the finance necessary for the tour of Europe.

TRG Management PLC are helping Miss McGovern by seeking sponsors to help pay her costs. Mr R P K Wolf-James, a director of TRG, said "Fiona is more than just a good golfer — she has world-class potential, and she has a great deal to offer sponsoring companies."

Assignment 3

Type the following names and addresses on address labels, on envelopes—or on paper cut to size to represent envelopes.

Mr T D Jemburn BS TD, 362 Pacifico Avenue, South Pasadena, CA 9130, USA

Mr V A Owaleda, YGA Textile Manufacturing Co Ltd PO Box 39, Port of Spain, Trinidad, West Indies

CONFIDENTIAL Mr G Walter O'Brannigan, 92 St Jude's Avenue, Belfast, BT7 4AQ

Miss B H Belleville-Ray, Flat 7, 439 Tooramie Road, Toorak, Victoria 3142, Australia

Mr C A Yeung, Cheong Hing Co Ltd, 313 Temple Road, Kowloon, HONG KONG

PERSONAL Professor T Guidy PhD MICE 62a Chalk Hill Lane, West Croydon, Surrey CRO 4DF

Alhaji J S Adejumobi, 42 Central Avenue, Bodija Estate, Ibadan, Nigeria

Chief A S Okunle, Box 4761, Ife Road, Lagos, Nigeria

Assignment 4

Type on A4 paper with margins of 20 and 80 Elite 12 Pitch (10 and 70 Pica 10 Pitch). Follow the line endings shown. Type abbreviations as shown. Find and correct 3 spelling errors.

Mr E G McDevitt, Secretary of the local branch of SENCIT, described the new group as an "umberella organisation" set up to achieve affective co-ordination of the efforts of the multifarious bodies helping senior citizens in the area.

The group is currently based at the Wigg Lane, Colbury, headquarters of the CCVS (Colbury Council for Voluntary Services). Mr McDevitt explained that the CCVS had helped to launch the SENCIT organisation in the district.

"The District Health Committee has just granted us representation on its Planning Team for the Elderly," he told us. "At presant SENCIT is funded mainly by the DHSS 'Opportunities for Volunteers Fund', but this source of finance is for a limited period only, and we shall soon have to rely on our own fundraising efforts."

Assignment 5

Proof-read the following passage and see how quickly you can identify 8 errors. Type a correct copy in 1½ line spacing, using blocked paragraphs.

```
Attention all householders in the Colbury district !  If you have

bulky household waste (eg, scrap D.I.Y. materials, old furniture,

garden rubbish) youcan take it to the to the County Council's free

disposal centres at Glendale Road or Abbey Lane.


    The centres are open every day of the week at the following

hours: Saturday - Thursday, 9.00 am - 5.00 pm; Friday, 9.00 am -

7.00 pm (May - September); Friday, 09.00 am - 4.00 pm (October -

April).


NB: The disposal centres now have facilities for re - cycling waste

oil, scrap paper and scarp metal.
```

Assignment 6

a. Leave . . . spaces after a full stop.

b. The punctuation style in which all unnecessary or 'decorative' punctuation is omitted, is known as . . . .

c. Which is the correct method of typing the time with the 12-hour clock?
    (i) 0430 pm   (ii) 4.30 pm   (iii) 430 pm   (iv) 4.30 p m

d. Which is the correct method of typing the time with the 24-hour clock?
    (i) 0830 am   (ii) 08.30 hours   (iii) 830 hours   (iv) 0830 hours

3 HEADINGS AND DISPLAY

Assignment 7

Use wide margins. Use paragraph headings, as shown.

FIRST AID TRAINING COURSES
For Factory and Office

<u>Introductory Course</u> This course is designed to teach students all aspects of practical First Aid, using materials provided in First Aid Boxes. To add realism, simulated injuries are used on the "casualties" on which the trainees practise.

<u>Refresher Course</u> Suitable for staff who have undertaken initial training, but who wish to revise their skills and learn the most up-to-date techniques.

<u>Appointed Persons Course</u> This course is organised to meet the needs of small businesses, where fully-qualified First Aiders are not required, but where a member of staff trained in emergency procedures is needed to comply with Health and Safety recommendations.

Assignment 8

Use wide margins. Change the paragraph headings to marginal headings.

FLORABUNDA PLANT ARRANGEMENTS
SPECIALLY DESIGNED TO ENHANCE YOUR OFFICE ENVIRONMENT

FELICITY A trough filled with a variety of silk plants and/or flowers in a range of sizes.

MARIANNA A large basket arrangement of silk flowers and plants.

CORINNA A large free-standing planter with a silk tree surrounded by green foliage plants.

ARIADNE A cascading hanging basket filled with flowers and foliage to create a splash of colour for any ceiling/wall area.

DENISE A pottery container filled with small silk plants and flowers suitable for brightening up the reception desk or any working area.

Assignment 9

Inset the paragraphs that are shown in capitals from the left and right margins. Capitalise as shown. Use wide margins. Find and correct 4 spelling errors.

FLORABUNDA PLANT ARRANGEMENTS

A new way to decorate your office

Are you looking for something different in office decor? Then we are sure you will be delighted with our lovely Florabunda Plant Arrangements, designed by award-winning florrists in a wide range of coulors and sizes.

    WE WILL DESIGN PLANTERS, TROUGHS, BASKETS, ETC, TO MATCH
    YOUR OFFICE DECOR OR YOUR COMPANY COULORS AT NO EXTRA COST.

Florabunda arrangements are solidly set in their containers so that they cannot be damaged in transit - or when you decide to move them around.

    WE CAN DESIGN ARRANGEMENTS TO FIT AN EXACT SPACE, OR AS A
    SCREEN, TO MEET YOUR EXACT REQUIREMENTS AT VERY LITTLE EXTRA
    COST.

Remember - silk flowers never wilt or droop, and occassional dusting is all the maintainance they need, so you save money in the long term.

Assignment 10

a. List at least 4 methods of emphasising headings so that they stand out from the rest of the text in a document.

b. Inset (or indented) items should be inset by at least . . . character spaces from the margin(s).

c. A paragraph in which the second and all following lines start 2 character spaces to the right of the first line is known as a . . . paragraph.

d. Marginal headings are sometimes called . . . headings.

Assignment 11

Type the following notice with shoulder headings and indented paragraphs as shown. Use wide margins.

SOUTHERN STAR HOLIDAYS
BOOKING CONDITIONS

Deposit

A deposit of £100 per person is payable when you confirm your reservation.

Travel Insurance

We strongly recommend that you purchase travel insurance at the time of booking.

Single Supplement

A single supplement must be paid where one person is travelling alone by choice.

Travel Documents

You are responsible for obtaining the appropriate visa(s). You must carry a valid passport at all times.

Refunds

No refund is available after the tour has commenced in respect of any trips, accommodation or meals not taken.

Assignment 12

The names in List 1 below will be used by the Florabunda company for new plant arrangements. The information has been repeated at the right in List 2. Compare and proof-read the lists and see how quickly you can spot 12 errors in List 2.

Then type List 1 correctly in alphabetical order of the names.

PLANT ARRANGEMENT NAMES	PLANT ARRANGEMENT NAMES
Imogen - bamboo trough	Imogen - bamboo troogh
Hildebrand - tiered planter	Hildebrand - teared planter
Philomena - decorative wheelbarrow	Phillomena - decorative wheel
Georgiana - circular planter	Georgina - circular planter
Anastasia - tall pottery vase	Anastasia - tall pottry vase
Myfanwy - large oval basket	Myfannwy - large oval basket
Wilhelmena - triple candlestick	Wilhelmena - triple candle stick
Brigitta - copper jug	Briggitta - copper jug
Catriona - small square basket	Katriona - small square basket
Johanna - pinewood trough	Joanna - pine-wood trough

4 PLACEMENT OF WORK ON THE PAGE AND TYPING FROM MANUSCRIPT

Assignment 13

Use paragraph headings. Type the main body of the text in double line spacing.

TELETEX [1] — sp. caps.

Teletex is a speedy, relatively inexpensive, method of communication [electronic mail] between computers and word processors, which has many benefits.

Speed A full page of A4 text can be transmitted to its destination within a few seconds.

Efficiency Messages can be stored during the day and sent out automatically during the cheaper rate periods overnight. One document can be sent automatically to a number of different recipients in locations.

Appearance Teletex has a full range of character sets and page formats, and documents retain the appearance of a normal typewritten page. [2]

TYPIST: Leave clear line spaces here for a diagram

International Access Teletex is an agreed international standard, and a computer in one country can communicate directly with another almost anywhere in the world.

(1) Sometimes called 'SUPER TELEX'. — l.c. with init. caps.

(2) Unlike Telex, wh. is restricted to capital letters and a restricted page format.

(3) International Telegraph and Telephone Consultative Committee.

Assignment 14

Match each of the following abbreviations in Column 1 with the correct meaning in Column 2.

Column 1		Column 2	
A	del'd	A	with
B	wh	B	should
C	tho'	C	through
D	info	D	which
E	shd	E	shall
F	cttee	F	department
G	thro'	G	though
H	sh	H	information
I	dept	I	committee
J	w	J	delivered

Assignment 15

Type in 1½ line spacing. Centre vertically on the page. Type all abbreviations in full. Find and
correct 4 spelling errors.

VERGREMONT CASTLE GARDENS — sp. caps

The gdns at V—— C—— offer a rich variety of botanical
specimens + beautiful vistas. The water gdns. incorporate
several pools, dotted w. islands, + filled w. ornemental
fish swimming gently among the water lilies. // The
Castle, wh. is the home of the present ~~Marquess of~~
Marchioness of V——, is open to the public from 1 May
to 30 Sept. There is a wooded picnic area by the
lake + secluded play areas for the children. The
tk tearoom, sighted in the old bake-house, provides
home-made fare. Souvenirs may be bought in the
Gift Shop, + plants are sold in the walled gdn. of
the C——.

Assignment 16

Compare the first paragraph with the second. See how quickly you can identify 13 differences in
the second paragraph. Then type paragraph 2 correctly, typing Plasti-Post in capitals wherever it
occurs, in 1½ line spacing.

Plasti-Post envelopes are better than ordinary paper envelopes. Less
weight means you pay less in postage charges. They are easier to handle
and quicker to pack and seal. Plasti-Post envelopes take up only a
quarter of the storage space of paper envelopes. In addition,
Plasti-Post envelopes are water-repellant and tough for maximum
protection.

Plasti-Post envelopes are much better than ordinry paper envelopes. Less
weigh means you pay less postage charges.They are easier to handle and
and quick to pack and seal. PlastiPost envelopes take up only about a
a quarter of the storeage space of paper envelopes. In addition,
Plasti-Post envelopes are also water-repellent and tough for the maximum
protection.

Assignment 17

Use single line spacing. Leave 2 clear line spaces at the points marked with an asterisk.

South Sea Islands Cruise ‾ Caps

Your Cruise Itinerary

*

SUNDAY: PAPEETE TO OPUNOHU BAY, MOOREA

The "Southern Empresse" leaves Papeete's busy and
colourful waterfront and crosses the "Sea of the

u.c. moon" to Moorea.

*

MONDAY: RAIATEA TO UTUROA

Over night the "Southern Empress" carries you to
the island of Raitea, fringed with coral reefs
and a blue lagoon. After a picnic lunch on the beach,
you cruise to Uturoa, with a chance to explore
this intriguing little town.

*

TUESDAY: UTUROA TO BORA BORA

By morning you will reach Bora Bora, and enjoy a day's
cruising in the lagoon.

l.c. In the evening you will be entertained by a typical
Tahitian Dance Group at a beach-side restaurant.

*

WEDNESDAY: TAHA'A TO HUAHINE

with a break for swimming + snorkelling in the lagoon

Taha'a will be waiting to greet you when you wake in
the morning. The morning will be spent cruising round
the entire island. In the late evening you reach
~~Faufea Bay in Ruiatea.~~ the lagoon of Huahine.

SNORKELLING:

swimming & snorkelling

PAPEETE

THURSDAY: HUAHINE TO ~~MOOREA~~

During the morning you cruise to d'Avea Bay for a lazy day. lunch is an u.c.
authentic Tahitian Feast prepared by local restaurant. The day is
rounded off by the Captains' Dinner, with floral garlands and dancing,
while the ship cruises through the night to arrive at Papeete at 8.00 am
on Friday morning.

Leave at least 65 mm (2½") of space here

Leave at least 65 mm (2½") of space here

5 CENTRED LAYOUT—HORIZONTAL CENTRING

Assignment 18

Use the block centred style of display. Centre horizontally and vertically on the page.

COMPUSCOTIA — sp. caps

COMPUTER SYSTEMS & COMMUNICATIONS CONSULTANTS

Communications Bureau
Microcomputers
Software Packages
uc. Word Processing systems
Prestel Telex Teletex

130-132 PERIVALE BLVD
GLASGOW G2 4RR

Double Line Spacing

Assignment 19

Justify the right margin. Type figures as shown.

Hilverdale Practice Aids — caps

for surgery, office and reception

Practice Account Book Loose-Leaf Sheets
uc. Income & expenditure
Analysis
Petty Cash & Wages
Daily Takings Sheet
Shedule Error Sheets
two General Anaesthetic Advice Cards
Receipt Book
Altered Appointment Card
Peelable Sterilizer Pouches
close up X-Ray Peel-Off Window Mount
X-Ray Mounting Strip
Waste Disposal Bags

25 Sheets
25 S —
30 S —
100-Sheet Pad
50-Sheet P—
500 Cards
Minimum 25 Books
500 C—, Unheaded
Reel of 250
Packet of 100
250 Pre-Cut Strips
Box of 250

Assignment 20

Centre each of the short items in the advertisement below. Justify the right margin of each of the paragraphs of text. Use wide left and right margins. Centre the display vertically on the page.

[Handwritten advertisement copy with editing marks:]

LINGUA: Lingua-Soft — Spaced Caps.

from

JEMMISON AUTOMATION

Jemmison Automation are the leading suppliers of integrated business software for microcomputers *i.e.* written in several European Languages.

[run on] Our software is designed to meet the needs of users all over the world, wherever these languages are spoken.

AVAILABLE IN

[1½ line spacing] *[two]* ENGLISH FRENCH GERMAN DUTCH   SPANISH PORTUGUESE ITALIAN

We can also supply software in "American English" with American spellings & terminology. Our brochure gives full details, & callers are welcome to examine — & try out — fully our range of microcomputer software.

THOUSANDS OF *[over 10,000 struck through]* USERS WORLDWIDE

[TYPIST: No underline]

Assignment 21

Proof-read the following passage and see how quickly you can identify 10 errors. Then type the passage, centring the heading on 3 lines and centring each of the short items.

```
FENSOME 'UPLIGHTERS' FOR INDIRECT LIGHTING IN YOUR OFFICE


Do your staff sufffer from eyestrain, headaches and glare?  Are
you using too much energy throuhg an inefficient lightning system?
Indirect lighting form FENSOME UPLIGHTERS offers:


                      Elegent designs
                    Modern color range
                    Simple re-location
                  Minimun standing space
                   Low installaton costs
                  Lowe maintainance costs
```

Assignment 22

Use margins of 24 and 88 Elite (20 and 70 Pica). Centre headings and other short items over the typing line. Find and correct 7 errors concerned with the use of apostrophes.

T R E N D & T R I M M E R (L T D) — in full

lc Proudly announce their appointment as

CAR
SPECIALIST FLEET/DEALER FOR GRIFFON CAR'S

leave 2 clear line spaces here

Our expertise in handling fleet operations both large and small, enables us to meet your needs precisely.

THE NORTHS' LEADING FLEET SPECIALISTS   over year's of experience

business
This specialised knowledge of day-to-day and long-term vehicle requirements has been built up and is now endorsed by Griffon cars themselves with this appointment.   new

uc

HIGHER
NEW CONTRACT HIRE AND LEASING SERVICE
LET US GIVE YOU A QUOTATION

We can meet your companys need's - whether you want just a few cars or a fleet of hundreds. Our specialist's will deal with your fleet enquiry's and tell you about the outstanding quality and unbeatable prices we offer.

Assignment 23

Use equal left and right margins. Justify items at the right margin.

Daniel Ireland — General Sales Manager
William Reece-Jones — Fleet Sales Manager
Fenjal Supri — Sales Executive
Louis Basque — Local Fleet Specialist
Samantha Hoosemain — Fleet Sales Controller
Alex Brittain — Fleet Service Specialist

Trend & Trimmer Ltd (in full) in Centre Caps
The North's Leading Fleet Service
Contact our Specialist Staff
for any
Fleet Enquiries on 061-222 76770

6 MEMOS

Assignment 24

Memo from Miss Heidi Clare, Word Processing Centre, to Mrs Vera Landon, Office Services Manager. Use memo-headed paper.

NEW COPY HOLDERS   *TYPIST* Close up "copy holders" throughout

Now that we have converted the Centralised Typing Section to the Word Processing Centre, the existing copy holders/used by/the typing pool for *wh. were* *staff in* several years, are proving unsatisfactory for the (wp) operators. ~~who are~~ *in full* *I have* *rec'd a number of complaints from operators* ~~complaining~~ of the awkward angle at which the copy must be placed with these copy holders, resulting/they claim/in neck-ache, eyestrain and fatigue. [I enclose a brochure giving details of electric*ally*-operated copy holders designed specially for use with VDUs. [If you agree to the purchase of/~~a~~ *these* new copy holders, I should like to try out the following ~~versions~~ *types* before a purchase is made, to see which/is most satisfactor*y*ly: *type* the table-top, the spring-arm and the clamp version. [Will you please let me know as soon as possible if you are able to arrange this.

Assignment 25

Use plain paper.

From Cedric Farrier, Sports & Social Club
To All Members of Staff
~~DOG~~ *puppy* TRAINING CLASSES
Is yr puppy driving you up the wall? Do/you/~~want~~ *wd like* to improve yr dog's behaviour? Do you ∧ have a "problem pet"? Are you willing to learn & ~~dogs~~ improve yr ability? (as a dog handler) [The Sports & Social Club has arranged a series of Dog Training Classes, to be held on Sat. mornings from 10.00 am to 11.30 am. [Interested? Contact Philip Mexborough on Ext 242 a.s.a.p.
(Want further details?)

Assignment 26

Use headed paper for this memo from John P Childers, Personnel Manager, to Sara Meacham, Training Department. Find and correct 4 grammatical errors.

FIRST AID TRAINING

As you are aware, the Health and Safety Executive has set up strict requirements for ensuring adequate levels of proficiency for First Aiders in offices and work-places. During the past year there has been several occasions when we have encountered difficulties in providing the correct level of cover, particularly during the summer holiday period.

Will you please arrange for a series of Training Sessions for First Aiders. We need urgently a course for new First Aiders. In addition we require some refresher class for people who have undertaken training in their previous employment but who have not taken up the role of First Aider with our company. Mr Ashuola has agreed that, if necessary, you may use the services of commercial training company. Let me have details as soon as possible.

Assignment 27

a. Name 2 items that are *not* included on a memo.

b. A symbol may be typed within the left margin of a memo to indicate that . . .

c. Name 3 items that are always included on a memo.

d. What details should be included at the head of the continuation sheet of a memo?

e. Name 3 items that are sometimes included on a memo.

Assignment 28

See how quickly you can find 13 errors in the following passage.

Memos may be typed on on pre-printed memo-headed paper or on on plain paper, depending on on the practice of the the company in which you work. work. Remember that you are you are always expected to insert the date, the date, even if you are not given instructions to do to do so. You should also insert an insert an appropriate reference, even if you are you are not told to do so. Always proofread your work and ensure that it it is accurate before you return it to it to the author for for signature.

Assignment 29

Type this memo from Mr G D Darling, Maintenance Dept, to All Heads of Dept. Use memo-headed paper for the first page and plain paper for the second page. Change paragraph headings to shoulder headings, and type all headings in capitals. Leave a clear line space between paragraphs.

Safety of Electric Plugs As requested by the Health and Safety Committee, I have conducted a thorough survey of the condition of electric plugs in the company's offices. A full report has been prepared for the H & S Cttee, but a summary of findings is given below for your information.

Incorrect Wiring Each plug was inspected for incorrect wiring, and we found that about 1.2% were faulty, mainly due to the reversal of positive and negative wires.

Condition of Plug Casing Each plug case was inspected for chips or cracks and missing screws, and 5.6% of the plugs had serious physical damage. Some of these were dangerous - one, in fact, was held together by clear adhesive cellulose tape. *(broken in half and was)*

Condition of Cord Grip The plugs were checked for condition of the cord grip, and 20% were found to be faulty. The main problems arose from missing/loose screws, and in some cases the cord grip was not in use at all.

Fuses Most plugs were fitted with a *It was found th.* 13 amp fuse, irrespective of the rating of the appliance being used. As almost 86% of the plugs were fitted with a 13 amp fuse when a lower rated fuse should be employed.

General Conclusions It is clear that the condition of electric plugs throughout the company's offices is most *Unsatisfactory* unsatisfactory, and that as all plugs are inspected and checked when equipment is installed, it is clear that members of staff are "tampering" with them at a later stage. The highest proportion of faults was found on "unauthorised" equipment such as private kettles and coffee-making machines.

RECOMMENDATIONS
(1)   A regular check should be instituted.
(2)   A clear policy that plugs and fuses are fitted and replaced only by maintenance staff, should be set up and adhered to.
(3)   "Unauthorised/private" appliances such as kettles, should be removed from all depts, *+ should not be replaced in future.*
(4)   All faulty plugs should be replaced immediately. (This is, in fact, being done.) *already under way.)*

Assignment 30

See how quickly you can find 10 errors in the following passage. Then type it correctly with a heading: COURTESY TITLES IN MEMOS.

It is not always necessary to include the courtesy title of the people sending and / or receiving a memo. Some companys always use the courtesy titles. Others have a more informal approach and memos may be sent, forexample, from "Fred Bolder" to "Josie Kane. Other people like to use the courtesy title for the recipient, but put there own name without one, e g, from "Don Pierce" to "Mr G w Heron". when you work in an office, follow the style used in your own Company

7 FILE COPIES

Assignment 31

Type this advertising leaflet, correcting 6 punctuation errors. Retain abbreviations. Take 1 carbon copy.

SOUTHERN REGION COMMERCE & INDUSTRY EXHIBITION —Centre

c — 8I —

Heres what some of our exhibitors said about last year's exhibition. u.c.

"A successful *and* well-organised exhibition which provided a perfect opportunity to meet local ~~industry~~ companies. We'll be back next year! CROSBIE COMPUTER SYSTEMS"

"This was the second time we participated   We *doubled* ~~increased~~ our stand space, *and* found ~~this~~ was well repaid because it enabled us to speak to many more; members of the business community. Chris Kerrie, Senior Information Officer, FDRC LIMITED"   (the increased expenditure)

"The exhibition provided an excellent number of quality leads. Many of these valuable leads have been successfully followed up and resulted in further business. SOUTHERN PERSONNEL & MANAGEMENT SERVICES LIMITED

"An unqualified success! "The exhibition provided us with a very high level of contacts and we immediately re-booked for next year with a much bigger stand. William Laughton Regional Sales Executive, CAPS Dragovend Limited"

The Exhibition will be given maximum publicity } Centre in Caps throughout the United Kingdom and overseas }

Assignment 32

a. What do the initials NCR stand for?

b. When a memo is copied or duplicated to be sent to a number of people, the list of names is known as the . . . list.

c. How can you identify copies of memos so that you know who is to receive each copy?

d. What do the initials 'bcc' stand for, and when is it used?

e. How can you identify the file copy of a memo?

f. What is the best position in which to type a "Bring Forward" note on a file copy?

Assignment 33

Use memo-headed paper. Take 1+3 carbon copies. Indicate distribution of the copies. Type all abbreviations in full.

From Miss D. Zachara, Personnel Dept
To Mrs S. A. Hamad, Editor, "Boden News"
Copy to ~~XXXXXX~~ Mr Clark Boden, Managing Director
Mr Bernard Boden

ITEM FOR "BODEN NEWS"

"Mr Bernard Boden has now joined the Company & will work his way thro' the firm, dept by dept., gaining valuable practical experience after his years of academic study. // Like his father & brother, Glen, Bernard was educated at Norgate College, Clifton, ~~there he gained~~ before gaining a BSc Honours degree in Accountancy & Managerial Studies at University College, Cardiff."

Please ensure that the folg. item appears in the next issue of the "Boden News".

Assignment 34

Compare the first paragraph with the second paragraph and see how quickly you can identify 15 differences in the second paragraph. Then type the first paragraph correctly in 1½ line spacing, taking 1 carbon copy. Use a centred heading WALKER BABY EQUIPMENT LIMITED.

Walker Baby Equipment Limited warrants that if any defect in materials or workmanship appears in the product within one year after the date of purchase, it will repair or replace the product free of charge. This applies only if the product has been used solely for domestic purposes and has not been damaged through misuse, accident or neglect, and has not been modified or repaired by anyone other than Walker Baby Equipment Limited. This warranty is in addition to the consumer's statutory rights and does not affect those rights in any way.

Walker Baby Equipment Limited warrantees that if any defect in material or work appears in the product within a year after the date of date of purchase, it will repair or replace the product free of charge. This applies only if the product has been used only for domestic purposes and has been damaged though mis-use, accident or neglect, and has not been modified or repaired by any one other than Walker Baby Equipment Company Limited. This is in addition to the consumers' statutory rights and does not effect those rights in anyway.

Assignment 35

Use memo-headed paper. Take 2 carbon copies.

On the carbon copies only type: BCC—Miss A Grey, Project Supervisor.

From Mr P D Pendry To Mr A G Farsi
Research Dept   Technical Director

NEW MULTI-PURPOSE SCOPES

In answer to the queries raised in your memo, Miss Grey
has provided the following information. (From the instrument)
A specially-designed programmable interface for the
instrument controllers ~~means~~ ensures that measurement
results are captured (for processing and analysis by
the controller. Accurate voltage and current
measurements are made using cross hair cursors and test
uc [a window mode displays minimum and maximum
limits in "GO/NO-GO" testing procedures. A sequencing mode automatically steps through a series of
test cycles without the help of a controller. Devices
sTe may also be [automatically ~~cycled~~ through tests]
under programme control.

Assignment 36

Memo from Mr G A Woodhead, Managing Director to Mr H Kemp, Public Relations Manager. To be
headed: Hemmanford Agricultural Show. On the file copy only, type a 'Bring Forward' note for the
copy to be brought forward a month from today—type in the appropriate date.

was   (an alternative to the marquee)
of course? As discussed with you, the Board ~~were~~ very disappointed with the quality of the company's
stand and marquee at the Hemmanford Show last week. The poor weather added to the
difficulties, ~~and~~ but it is obvious that we need ~~some improvement~~ for next year's show.

A friend of mine mentioned that Fleetgood Caravans in Abberley hire out prestige caravan
s units for use at 'hospitality suites' at shows of this kind. I understand ~~that~~ they are
supplied complete with integral kitchen, bar and ~~comfortable~~ seating area. If necessary, a
generator can also be hired.

Please contact Fleetgood and let me have your opinions on the suitability of one, or perhaps
two, of these caravans for our purposes. It might be an idea to try out one of the units at
lc the Foreham Flower Show as an experiment. Let me know what the costs would be, as soon as
possible.   (Have a look at the caravans personally &)

8 LISTS, NUMBERS AND MEASUREMENTS

Assignment 37

The use of words/figures and the method of representing measurements is inconsistent in the following passage. Find and correct 6 inconsistencies, and then type the passage correctly. Leave a clear line space between paragraphs.

BATIKA ALUMINIUM GREENHOUSES — Centre

1 Generous 4' 9" eaves height (9" higher than any of our competitors' makes).
2 Straight sides to give more room for plants. [tall]
3 Standard sizes: 6' 2" x 6' 2"; 6' 2" x 8' 0"; 6' 2" x 10' 2½";
   6' 2" x 12' 3"; 6' 2" x 14' 3½" and 6' 2" x 16' 0" long.
4 All glass is 24 oz (3 mm) thick, horticultural grade, 24 inch x 24"
5 Built-in 2½ inch guttering and condensation channels along the two longer sides.
7 Roof-opening ventilators can be positioned wherever desired along the ridge bar. One window is provided for sizes 6' 2" - 8', two windows for sizes 10' 2½" - 12' 3", and 4 windows for 14' 3½" - 16 ft sizes.
6 Free staging for all 6'2" by 16'0" greenhouses.

Assignment 38

Use single line spacing.

IMPROVING EFFICIENCY

← leave 2 clear line spaces here

1 NEED FOR TRAINING

A recent survey claimed that over 80% of microcomputer users cd. gain more benefit from their computer. Three areas were highlighted:

  1.1 Move training by experienced + qualified staff.
  1.2 Better training, more specifically related to company needs.
  1.3 Increased practice time following training courses.

[NO line space between paras.]

← leave 2 clear line spaces here

2 MAJOR USES

The survey revealed that the 4 major uses of executive microcomputers, were as listed below:

  2.1 Perhaps surprisingly, the major use was for spreadsheets + financial applications.
  2.2 Word proc'g was the next highest use.
  2.3 Relatively few users made extensive use of graphics programs.
  2.4 Database management was widely used.

[NO line space between paras.]

Assignment 39

Use double line spacing for the main body of the text and single line spacing for the inset
paragraphs.

KIRKWARDLE

HIRING FAIR AT BARFIELD AGAIN

For the fifth time our Barfield Depot provided temporary floodlighting
for the Barfield Hiring Fair so that Visitors would be sure to see all
the high lights of this popular event. We were asked to provide A total
of 32 Mobile 'Towerlights', which were strategically positioned to
provide security operations and to illuminate carpark entries and
walkways throughout the Fair site. each 21.35 m high,

Five of our engineers were stationed on the site throughout the four
days of the Fair to oversee the delivery and erection of the Towerlights
and provide a full maintenance service.

INSET FROM LEFT AND RIGHT MARGINS

Barfield Hiring Fair was first held in 1284 under a right
conferred by Edward I. The principal activity in those days
was the hiring of agricultural and domestic labour, together
with the sale of poultry and vegetable products. 3.2 km from the city centre,

The Fair moved to its present site at the Garston Park, in 1932.
Today's Hiring Fair provides dozens of modern fairground rides,
plus over a hundred sideshows and stalls for the 500,000 or
more people who visit the fair every year. 100-150

In Over the last few years we have also been asked to provide temporary office
accommodation and mobile toilets for the administration centre. These con-
sisting of two portable units 9.75 m x 3.05 m for use by First Aid
staff, a 7.35 m x 2.75 m office used by the organisers as a retrieval
point for lost children. We also supplied four of our 5.80 m main toilet
units for use by the many thousands of people who visited the fair.

Assignment 40

The information in list one is correct. The details have been repeated in list two at the right.
Compare the lists and see how quickly you can identify 15 errors. Then type list one correctly,
putting the items in alphabetical order, using double line spacing.

List one	List two
SPECIFICATION	SPECIFICATION
Machine deckle: 6,600 mm	Machine deckled: 6,600 mm
Grammage range: 60 g/m^2 to 135 g/m^2	Grammage range; 60 g/m^3 to 135 g/m^2
Reel widths: min 200 mm, max 2,400 mm	Reel widths: min 20 mm, max 2,400 mm
Reel diameters: 800 mm and 1,000 mm	Reel diamters: 800 mm and 1000 mm
Boxes per pallet: 40 (500 kg) and 80 (1,000 kg)	Boxed per pallett: 40 (500 kg and 80 (1,000 kg)
Reams per box: A4 - 5 or 10	Reams per box: A5 - 5 kg or 10 kg
Wrapping: White 90 g/m^2 bleached kraft	Wrapping White 90 g/m bleached kraft

Assignment 41

Use memo-headed paper. Use marginal headings as shown. Take 1 carbon copy. On the carbon copy type a 'Bring forward' note for the copy to be brought forward at the end of this month (give the appropriate date—make sure you give a weekday date, not Saturday or Sunday).

Memo from John Danvers to Alex Cinnamond
Will you pl. arrange for the foll.g. advertisement to be
placed in the next issue of "Industrial Propperty Monthly".
HOLT-HIGHLANDS PROPERTY (COMMERCIAL DEPT
(a) PAISLEY Nantfield Lane. Warehouse & offices —
48,000 sq ft. Site area 1.55 acres.
£275,000 subject to contract.
(b) RENFREW Corby Road Indust. Estate. Newly-built
warehouse/indust. units on established
estate. Steel Portal frame 16ft 6in
eaves. A variety of units to let — 4,000
sq ft, 5,400 sq ft, 6,570 sq ft or
14,800 sq ft. From £8.50/sq ft.
(c) GLASGOW Hamish St. W'house & offices,
with car park for over 200 cars.
61,000 sq ft. Site area 2 acres.
£295,000 subject to contract.

Assignment 42

a. What number is represented by the roman numeral viii?

b. How many character spaces should be left after paragraph numbers?

c. Superscript characters are those that are typed . . . the normal line of type.

d. Subscript characters are those that are typed . . . the normal line of type.

e. Name 2 metric units that are usually typed in full to avoid confusion and/or error.

f. The style of paragraph labelling that uses the numbering system 1, 1.1, 1.1.1, 2, 2.1, 2.2.1, etc, is known as the . . . numbering system.

Assignment 43

Type abbreviations as shown. Centre horizontally and vertically on the page.

MEXILANA OPTICAL DISK DRIVE ← *PHYSICAL SPECIFICATIONS*

Environmental Limits

Ambient temperature: 50 $^\circ$F to 109 $^\circ$F (10 $^\circ$C to 43 $^\circ$C).

l.c. Relative Humidity: 10% to 90%.

l.c. Maximum Wet Bulb: 80 $^\circ$F (26.7 $^\circ$C).

DC Voltage Requirements

+15 V DC @ 4 A peak. ± 5 %
-15 V DC @ 4 A peak. ± 5 %
+5 V DC @ 14 A peak. ± 5 %

1½ line spacing here

Error Rates

errors:

Non-recoverable 1 per 10^{12} bits read.   Non-detected errors: 1 per 10^{16}
bits read.
Seek errors: 1 per 10^6 seeks.

1½ line sp.

Dimensions   *TYPIST: List these items in 1½ line spacing*

Height: 6.81" (173.0 mm). Width: 17.6" ~~inches~~ (447.0 mm). Depth: 24"
(609.6 mm). Weight: 50 lb (27.7 kg).

Assignment 44

Use double line spacing for the paragraphs. Leave 3 clear line spaces between paragraphs. Correct any inconsistencies. Leave 11 clear line spaces between the first paragraph and sub-paragraph (i).

Australian Safari Treks by Motor Caravan — Caps & Centred

(i) The Southern Fringe Route crosses Australia between Perth & Sydney (3961 km/1745 miles). The cost per person is A$795.00.

(ii) The Traveller Route runs between Adelaide & Perth, across the Nullarbor Plain (2,663 km/1,664 miles) (2857 km/1786 miles) for A$620.25 per person.

(iii) The Springs Route between Sydney & Alice Springs costs A$620.25 per person.

(iv) The Trans-Australia makes the (1,861 km/1,050 miles) journey between Brisbane ~~South~~ & Cairns for only A$495.50 per person.

(v) The Adelaide–Alice route runs from Adelaide to Alice Springs (1553 km/971 m). The cost p.p. is A$395.50 ~~per person~~.

Try a Safari Trek holiday across Australia by motor caravan. Nothing you have ever done before will compare with this holiday of a lifetime!

9 FORMS

Assignment 45

Type this form. When completed and checked, remove it from the typewriter and retain it for use in Assignment 46.

FLYTEPARK PARK-AND-RIDE AIRPORT SERVICE

Name .... Surname ......
Address ....
u.c. Postcode ...... Telephone ....
u.c. Make of car ...... Model ......
Colour ...... Registration ......
Date Outward ..... Destination ....
Time of Flight ...... Flight Number ...
Date of ~~Re-tu~~ Return ..... Returning from ...
Flight Arrival Time ...... Flight No ...
Number of ~~People in Party~~ Adults ..... No of Children ...
No. of Days ...... Indoor/Outdoor Parking*
Please arrive at Flyte House 2 hours before flight time.
Please reserve car parking and transport
to/from ~~the~~ airport.
* Please delete as appropriate.
Signed ...... Date ....

Typist: All these lines to end at same point.

Assignment 46

Complete the form you typed for Assignment 45 with the following details. The information is not provided in the order required for completing the form—select the details as necessary. The form is to be completed ready for signature today.

Mr Brian Mackenzie, his wife and 3 children of 402 Glasberrie Road Port Talbot SA12 4JB (Telephone 06396-44217) are travelling to Boston, USA. Date of outward flight:) 16 July Flight number: BA275 departing at 1630 hours They are returning from Boston, USA, on 30 July on Flight Number BA274, arrival time 0810 hours. Mr Mackenzie has a red Vauxhall, Astra 1300s, registration number C 746 HRG, and he requires indoor parking for 14 days.

ASTRA

26

Assignment 47

Find and correct 6 spelling errors. Type all abbreviations in full. Retain the completed form for use in Assignment 48.

INSTITUTE OF CRAFT TECHNICIANS

ANNUAL CONFERANCE   *Centre*

"UNUSUAL OBJECT" COMPETITION

You are invited to display an "unusual object" on the competition table *to*
during the Conferance from 1600 hours on Friday, 14 April, ~~and~~ 1300 hrs on
Saturday, 15 April. You may display as many objects as you wish, but each
object must be entered on a seperate entry form. **Please note that,
although every effort will be made to safegaurd exibits, ~~it must be
stressed that~~ objects are displayed at the owner's risk and ~~that~~ no
responsability can be accepted ~~by the organisers~~ for loss or breakage.

l.c. Mr Andrew Currie and Mr Leon Vila, members of the North-East Regional
Cttee, will judge the competition, and the ~~winner~~ will be presented with a
matched set of Darley Suitcases. The result of the competition will be
announced at the Dinner Dance on Saturday evening, *when the winner
will be expected to explain what the object is.*

Centre ENTRY FORM *-sp.caps*   *person judged to have entered
the most unusual object*
"UNUSUAL OBJECT" COMPETITION

Name ....
Address ....
....
Region ....
Membership Number ....

BRIEF DISCRIPTION OF THE OBJECT — *Centre*

....
....

*TYPIST Draw a box here at least 38 mm
(1½) deep. Align left & right ruling of box
with start & finish of items in the form section.*

Assignment 48

Complete the form you typed for Assignment 47 with the following details.

Jennifer Holmeswood of 39 Silver Bay Road, Cockermouth, Cumbria, CA13 9TQ, a member of the North-West Region is entering an unusual object. Her brief description is as follows: A small bundle of 6 irregularly-shaped wooden sticks, each stick about 14 mm long by 10mm wide, flat on one side and roughly shaped on the other, the bundle secured by 'raffia' string. Memb. No. 431699

Assignment 49

Type the invoice form shown below. Retain the completed form for use in Assignment 50.

ROAD-READY AUTO SERVICE CENTRE LIMITED
12a Cross Anchor Street
GALASHIELS
TD1 7EX
Telephone: 0896—337766l
VAT Registration Number 414/7677/310

INVOICE — sp caps

Customer _____
Address _____

Date _____
Invoice Number _____
Vehicle _____
Registration No _____

REPAIRS	TOTAL
↑ Leave at least 100 mm (4") here	£
TOTAL PLUS VAT TOTAL DUE	

Assignment 50

Complete the invoice form with the following details.

The customer is Mrs G Ardrossan, 3 Valley Road, Galashiels. Today's date. Invoice Number 7764. Vehicle – Talbot Horizon, Registration Number B 416 AGR. Insert the TOTAL DUE figure.

To replacing offside brake pipe, nearside front side-light bulb, offside rear brake light bulb, releasing handbrake and blowing out rear drums and brake shoes.

Materials		
Copper Brake Pipe	4.25
Brake Fluid	2.50
2 Light Bulbs @ 0.55	1.10
2 Unions @ 0.75	1.50

Carrying out MOT Test	10.00
Labour – 2½ hours	23.75
TOTAL	43.10
VAT	6.47

Assignment 51

Type the following form on card measuring 152 mm × 102 mm (6″ × 4″) or on A4 paper folded twice to approximately those measurements. Address the *reverse* side of the card to The Primavera House Hotel, FREEPOST, Regents Park, London, NW1 4JK. In the top right-hand corner type FREEPOST.

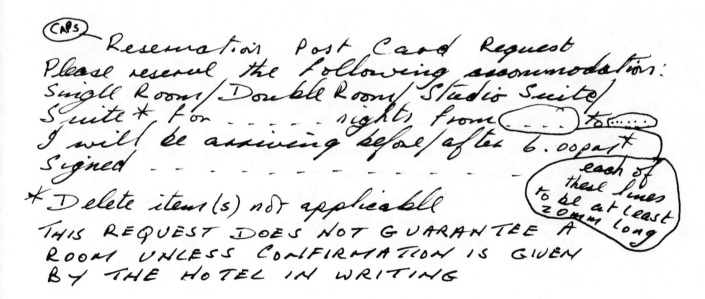

(CAPS) Reservation Post Card Request

Please reserve the following accommodation:

Single Room / Double Room / Studio Suite / Suite * for ...... nights from (......) to (......)

I will be arriving before / after 6.00pm *

Signed - - - - - - - - - - - - - - -

each of these lines to be at least 20mm long

* Delete item(s) not applicable

THIS REQUEST DOES NOT GUARANTEE A ROOM UNLESS CONFIRMATION IS GIVEN BY THE HOTEL IN WRITING

Assignment 52

See how quickly you can find 15 errors in the information on the following card. Then type a correct copy of the form on a card. Address the reverse side to Circulation Department, Office Equipment Listing, 35 Daisybrooke Street, Failsworth, Manchester, M35 9BT.

```
Please send me OFFICE EQUIPEMENT LISTING FREE EACH Month

Name ........................ Job tittle ................

Companyname ..................,,...........................

Buisness address .........................................

.............................Postcode ...................

My company ' s line off business ........................

number of employeees .....................................

Singed ...................... date .......................
```

Assignment 53

a. Use . . . line spacing for sections of a form containing the insertion lines.

b. Use . . . to type the "tear-off" line for a "tear-off slip".

c. Should the "tear-off" line be typed from margin to margin or from edge to edge of the paper?

d. Allow an insertion line of at least . . . long for a name.

e. Allow an insertion line of at least . . . for a date and at least . . . for a telephone number.

f. Use either the . . . or the . . . to type the insertion lines on a form.

Assignment 54

Type the following memo on headed paper. Take 1 carbon copy.

Memorandum from Mr L G Brendan, Engineering Department to All Gardening Section Members, Staff Sports & Social Club.   VISIT TO MEOLSFORD HALL GARDENS

I have organised an evening excursion to Meolsford Hall Gdns on 29 June. This visit will include a guided tour round the gdns by Lord Meolsford himself, ~~followed by~~ and a light buffet meal in NP the Conservatory at the end of the tour. [The cost of the ~~visit~~ excursion is £7.50, including the coach fare. The pick-up point for the coach is the Drinkwater Hotel on Goode St.]

[Only 28 places are available, & places will be allocated on a 'first-come-first-served' basis. [Please complete the reply slip below, & return it to me a.s.a.p.

To Mr L G Brendan, Eng. Dept.
VISIT TO MEOLSFORD HALL GDNS
NP Please reserve a place for me on the excursion to M — H — G— on 29 June. [I enclose a cheque for £7.50.   Retain Abbvns
Name
Department   Tel Extn

10 DOTS, ACCENTS AND BRACKETS

Assignment 55

Type the following memo, using square brackets where shown. Take 1 carbon copy.

Memo from Arnold Garthwaite [Mg. Director] to All Members of Technical Staff. Heading WASTE METAL RETRIEVAL. [CAPS] It is essential that (all) forms of waste material that [lower case] may contain precious metals [dowel, grindings, bench sweepings, floor sweepings, dust from extractor bags and face masks] shd. be collected at the end of each day's work and placed in the blue collection bin [please ensure that the bin contains about a (inert) [before depositing the waste]]. [N.P.] Failure to carry out this routine is regarded as a serious disciplinary matter [as agreed w. the Union Representatives (see section VI of Conditions of Service)].

At the end of each month, 25% of the payment rec'd for waste metal will be distributed to ~~workshop~~ technical staff [with deductions for days of absence (see Section IX of Condns. of Service) excluding holiday entitlement].

RETURN THIS SLIP TO MR A SMARTHWAITE IMMEDIATELY to ~~CONFIRM~~ AS A CONFIRMATION OF RECEIPT

GRAPPENLINK LABORATORIES
WASTE METAL RETRIEVAL NOTICE

I confirm receipt of the WASTE METAL [CAPS] retrieval notice issued on . . . .

Name . . . .

Employee Number . . . .

Signature . . . . Date . . . .

Section . . . .

Assignment 56

Use leader dots. Justify the right margin.

Assignment 57

Identify and correct 5 spelling errors. Use indented paragraphs. *Do not* type a separating line between the main body of the text and the footnote. Use a centred heading: FREE 15-MONTH WALL PLANNING CHART.

Assignment 58

Type this contents page in double line spacing. Use leader dots in groups of 2 dots and 3 spaces. Justify the right margin. Do not use dittos—type the words in full. Centre horizontally and vertically on the page.

ROBO-WRITER USER MANUAL

CONTENTS

TYPIST leave an extra line space between main items

Page

1	INTRODUCTION	1
2	OPERATION	
	2.1 General	3
	2.2 Logging-on and Logging-off	5
	~~2.3 Creating New Files~~	~~6~~
	2.45 General Housekeeping Operations	810
	2.3 Creating New Files	6
	2.4 " a Security Back-Up Copy	8
3	TEXT FORMATTING	
	3.1 ~~The~~ Margins, Linespacing and Tabs	12
	3.2 Centring, Justifying Text " Emboldening	15
4	PAGE ~~COMMANDS FORMATTING~~ COMMANDS	
	4.1 ~~Page Formatting~~ Headers and Footers	18
	4.2 " " — Chapter Numbering	21
	4.3 " " — Commands	23
5	PRINTING	
	5.1 Printing from File	26
	5.2 " " Screen	29
6	ERROR MESSAGES	[31]
7	GLOSSARY OF TERMS	[33]

Assignment 59

The items in the menu on the left have been correctly typed. See how quickly you can find 10 differences in the menu on the right. Then type the menu shown on the left, centring each line and displaying effectively on the page.

GOURMET BUFFET MENU

La Soupe de Crème Colombine
Les Bouchées de Champignons
La Tranche de Poissons Fumés
Le Poulet de Grain en Gelée
Le Carré de Porc sous Croûte
Fraises a la Crème
Zabaglione aux Pêches
Les Gâteaux et Patisseries
Café et les Petits Fours

Chef: François Maçon

GOURMET BUFFET MENU

La Soup de Crème Colombine
Les Bouchées de Champgnons
La Tranche de Poissons Fumées
Le Poule de Grain en Gélee
Le Carré de Porc sous Cruste
Fraises A la Crème
Zabaglione aux Peaches
Les Gâteaux est Patisseries
Café et les Petits Fours

Chief: François Maçon

Assignment 60

Type the following wine list. Use wide margins. Follow the style of leader dots shown. Centre
horizontally and vertically on the page.

THE GOLDEN CUPRESSUS RESTAURANT

W I N E   L I S T

BORDEAUX

Château la Louvière	£9.25
Médoc	£7.25

RHINE

Bereich Schloss Böckelheim	£6.25
Rüdesheimer Rosengarten	£6.45
Oppenheimer Krötenbrunnen	£6.15

LOIRE

Saumur Cuvée des Plantagenets	£6.49
Muscadet, Château de la Galissonnière	£6.65
" de Sèvre-et-Maine	£6.35
Anjou Rosé	£6.15

RHÔNE

Côtes du Rhône	£6.15
Châteauneuf-du-Pape Domaine de Cabrières	£9.45

SPAIN

Viña Esmerelda	£7.25
Viña Herminia	£6.55

Include leader dots for all other wines please

Leave 2 clear line space here

Assignment 61

Type the names of staff in lower case with initial capitals. Type in alphabetical order of sections.
Put staff names in alphabetic order of surname in each section. Centre horizontally and vertically.

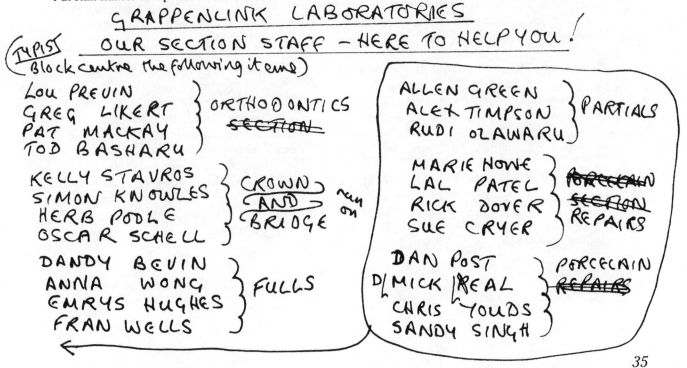

GRAPPENLINK LABORATORIES

OUR SECTION STAFF - HERE TO HELP YOU!

(TYPIST) (Block centre the following items)

LOU PREVIN
GREG LIKERT   } ORTHODONTICS
PAT MACKAY   } ~~SECTION~~
TOD BASHARU   }

KELLY STAVROS
SIMON KNOWLES   } CROWN
HERB PODLE   } AND
OSCAR SCHELL   } BRIDGE

DANDY BEVIN
ANNA WONG   } FULLS
EMRYS HUGHES
FRAN WELLS

ALLEN GREEN
ALEX TIMPSON   } PARTIALS
RUDI OLAWARU

MARIE HOWE
LAL PATEL   } ~~PORCELAIN~~
RICK DOVER   } ~~SECTION~~
SUE CRYER   } REPAIRS

DAN POST
D/MICK REAL   } PORCELAIN
CHRIS YOUDS   } ~~REPAIRS~~
SANDY SINGH

Assignment 62

a. Leader dots may be typed in a number of styles. Give 2 examples.

b. The abbreviation *do* or the sign " may be used to represent the word . . ., to indicate that . . .

c. "Ellipsis" is shown in typewriting by the use of . . .

d. If special keys are not available on the typewriter, accents should be inserted by . . .

e. How is the brace represented in typewriting?

Assignment 63

Follow the layout indicated. Use double line spacing for the paragraphs and single line spacing for the listed items.

THE BEST OF OUR SUMMER WINE —Centre

we attach our latest (. . .)

~~This~~ wine list ~~is~~ a simple guide to our wide and varied selection of wines from the best wine-producing countries in the world.

TYPIST indent these sections from the left and right margins

Loire
Rhône
Alsace
Beaujolais
Burgundy
Mâconnais-Chalonnais
Chablis
Côte d'Or
Bordeaux
} France

Rhine
Moselle
} Germany

Italy
Spain
Portugal
Austria
Hungary
Yugoslavia
Bulgaria
Greece
California
Australia
Lebanon
Chile

These items in alphabetical order and justified at the right.

If you have any problems or queries, simply contact our helpful staff in your local Cadillo wine shop ... they are always ready to give you the benefit of their knowledge and experience. ~~Our specialist~~ services u.c. ~~include:~~ provided in our

Fully-trained ~~and experienced~~ staff
Sale or return facilities
Free glass loan scheme
Generous quantity discounts
Specialist advice ~~and guidance~~
Fully party service
Local deliveries
Wine tasting evenings

Free l.c.

~~We have~~ 650 shops in towns and cities across the country include:

All prices include VAT at 15% and are correct as at (TYPIST insert today's date), but we reserve the right to change them without notice. Customers ordering a case of 12 bottles of wine (which may be in mixed cases) ~~is~~ are entitled to a discount of 5% off shelf prices . . . provided the wine is not on a special promotional offer.

11 BUSINESS LETTERS

Assignment 64

Use letter-headed paper. Take 1 carbon copy. Type an envelope.

Mr H W Yarrow, Advertising Manager, Purple Thistle Radio PLC, PO Box 276, Carrick Street, Edinburgh EH2 4BB

Dear Mr Yarrow

(introductory)

Thank you for your help with our first advertising campaign with ~~total~~ Purple Thistle Radio, which has proved very successful. The response ~~from~~ to our offer from small companies in the region has been tremendous, and this has opened up a new market for our loading equipment. ~~It~~ We hope to run a similar campaign towards the end of the year — when we have ~~increased~~ re-organised our Production Dept to cope with the increase in orders.

yrs ssly

Assignment 65

Use letter-headed paper. Take 1 carbon copy. Type an envelope.

Our ref GO'C/CHGF/47/17B

Mr P Vegas, Group Hire Manager, Stackington-Price Ltd,
7-9 Gooch Road, Bathgate, EH48 1TS.

Dear Mr Vegas
    I write to thank you and everyone else involved at Stackington-Price Ltd for the first-class service provided at the Highland Games Festival [last month] held by our company to celebrate our Centenary. //The whole event went off with scarcely a hitch, and your staff are to be congratulated for this very fine achievement, and for the friendly and efficient manner in which they carried out their work. //You can be sure that we shall recommend your services to any colleagues who are ~~considering~~ [planning] an event of this kind.
    Yours sincerely
    HIE-LAND INDUSTRIES LIMITED
    Gordon O'Connell
    PUBLIC RELATIONS MANAGER

For yr interest I enclose a copy of our House Magazine, which contains a 10-page "spread" on the Games.

Assignment 66

Type this standard circular letter on letter-headed paper. For the date type *Date as Postmark*. Do not leave a space for the inside address. Leave a space for the writer's signature. Type the enclosure details as shown.

Our ref PSB/FD

Dear Sir

Thank you for yr enquiry concerning our TMG/Huger products. We have pleasure in enclosing a copy of our booklet "Guide to Central Heating", together w. details of TMG/Huger central heating programmers, type Hugotrol 90 and 95M.

The Hugotrol 90 is for use w. gravity-fed systems, and the 95M for installations where motorised valves are to be controlled.

NP At the back of the booklet is a £10 voucher, redeemable from any distributor of Hie-land central heating products.

NP For yr convenience we also enclose a list of ~~our product details~~ distributors. However, if you have any difficulty in obtaining TMG/Huger equipment, we sh. be pleased to supply yr requirements direct against a cheque or VISA/ACCESS settlement. If you choose to pay by cheque, please complete the attached card and return it to us with yr order.

Yrs fly

HIE-LAND INDUSTRIES LIMITED   or credit card

Philip S Bootson

MARKETING MANAGER

Encs   1) Hugotrol 90/95M data sheet
         2) List of ~~stockists~~ distributors
         3) Card for cheque/~~VISA~~ VISA/ACCESS settlement
         4) "Guide to Central Heating" booklet with £10 voucher

and the £10 voucher

38

Assignment 67

Type the following form letter on letter-headed paper. Leave at least 38 mm (1½″) for the date and name/address of the addressee to be inserted later. Leave space for variable details to be inserted in the body of the letter at the appropriate points. Leave space for Mrs Danvers' signature.

Our ref BJD/SDW

Dear

CHANGE OF APPOINTMENT

I confirm the following changes in your employment, as discussed at our ~~meeting~~ on *annual staff review interview*

(Inset from left margin)

New post

Branch

Department

New salary

l.c. Car User Grade

These changes are effective from   . *I enclose a copy of the revised conditions of service for this post.* u.c.

May I take this opportunity of thanking you for your efforts during the past year, and wish you every success in your new appointment.

Yours faithfully
HIE–LAND INDUSTRIES LIMITED

BRIDGET J DANVERS
Chief Personnel Manager

Assignment 68

Complete the form letter typed in Assignment 67 with appropriate details selected from the information given below.

Letter to Miss Kirsty Darwen, 49 South Crumsden Road, ~~Glas~~ Glasnevin, Edinburgh, EH7 4MX. New post - Technical Support Manager at Darlington, Technical Services Dept. New Salary £14,395 Car User Grade - VI. The Meeting was held on Tuesday, with changes effective from 1st of next month - but put in the appropriate dates please.

Assignment 69

Use letter-headed paper for the first sheet of this letter, and plain matching paper for the second page. Take 1 carbon copy. Change the paragraph headings to shoulder headings. Type an envelope.

Miss R A Pringle, 52a Brook Buildings, Baxter Street, SCARBOROUGH, North Yorkshire, YO11 3VK.   Our ref BJD/CDA.

PROFESSIONAL WORK PLACEMENT

Dear Miss P, As agreed with your tutors, we shall be happy to accept you at Hie–Land House for your six-month Professional Work Placement period.

I enclose a brochure, which gives an outline of the company's history and development. ~~during the past 100 years.~~ As you are probably aware, we are currently celebrating the Centenary of the founding of the company. The brochure also gives details of the many and varied products we manufacture and sell, and I hope this will be of use in the preparation of your background notes for your thesis.

I have now worked out a provisional programme for you, and have tried to relate this to the ~~your your~~ main areas of interest (as far as possible) in your degree course.   An outline of the programme is given below, and a detailed schedule will be given to you on arrival.

MONTH ONE The first two weeks will be spent in the Publicity and Public Relations Department. This will help you to gain some background to the workings of the company before you move into the other departments. The second two weeks will be spent in the Advertising Department.

MONTH TWO Your second month will be spent in the Accounts Department, gaining an insight into the computerised accounting system used by the company.

MONTH THREE Although production control is not specifically mentioned in your tutor's request, we feel that you would benefit from a month spent in our Production Control Department, which has a central co-ordinating function in the company.

MONTH FOUR Your ~~fourth~~ you month will be spent 2 weeks in the Central Purchasing Dept, and the rest of the month in the Sales Dept.

MONTH FIVE Your period with the Central Training Department will involve you in a variety of ways. You will be given experience of the organisation and operation of the Central Training Dept, and may perhaps be called upon to act as an Instructor/lecturer for some of our courses for office staff. Towards the end of the month you will take part, as a trainee, in the Sales Courses, as a preparation for your period spent in the Sales Dept.

MONTH SIX You will spend one week with me in the Central Personnel Dept, before returning to the Accounts Dept, where you will be able to take a more informed interest in the operation and functions of this department in the light of your experiences throughout the previous 5 months.

I think this programme will give you a varied and valuable insight into the operation of a large organisation. If there are any changes you would like to make, please let me know as soon as possible, and I shall do my best to incorporate your ideas.

My secretary, Miss Vince, will be writing to you within the next week or so with details of arrangements for your accommodation while you are in Edinburgh. We look forward to meeting you.

Yours sincerely, HIE–LAND INDUSTRIES LIMITED, Bridget J Danvers, Chief Personnel Mgr.

Assignment 70

Use letter-headed paper and the semi-blocked layout style. Take 2 carbon copies. On the carbon copies only, type: Copy to Mr S Torres, Technical Support Department. Identify the carbon copies ready for distribution.

Our ref BGO/IPG42/SK
Your ref LRGG/SY

Mr L R G Goodison, Travos (UK) PLC, Travos Hse, 77 Bruce Ave, Edinburgh EH2 4WD

Dear Mr Goodison

INFORMATION SYSTEMS MEETING

As arranged, I enclose a copy of the notice we have circulated to our members and other interested people — about the meeting on Thursday, 27 January.

I confirm that we are satisfied, for the purposes of the demonstration, if you connect two of your facsimile machines. Mr Torres, of Technical Support Dept, will be present, & will give you any assistance you need.

We expect your demonstration to take place between 6.45 pm & 7.45 pm. If you wd like to hear Colin Tinsdale's talk at 5.30 pm, we shd be happy for you to arrive early enough to set up your equipment before he begins. Please let me know what time you expect to arrive. We will not know exactly how many people will be attending until nearer the date, but expect it to be around 35-40 people.

Yrs sincerely
Basil Ormerod
Secretary
Staff Information Systems Club

Assignment 71

Type the following letter on plain white paper. Type the sender's address—Allegra Cottage, Russell Avenue, Falkirk, FK4 7QQ, Telephone 0324-776478—across the top of the page. Use wide margins. Identify and correct 9 spelling errors in the letter.

Miss Johanna Carnegie, 1774 South Lake Drive, PEORIA, Illinois 61622 USA.

Dear Miss Carnegie, I saw your advertisement in the local newspaper ~~in connection with~~ about your research into your family conections with Falkirk. As I have made a hobby of traceing my family history, I have gathered together quiet a collection of information about the Carnegie family/ies in Falkirk. Their is every likelyhood that details of your ~~family~~ ancestors are recorded in the ~~records~~ material I have amassed. If you will send me further ~~details~~ information to suppliment the brief details in your advertisement, I shall be happy to try to trace relevant references in my notes. I look forward to hearing from you.

Yours sinserely, Alexander Firth-Carnegie

Assignment 72

See how quickly you can identify 12 errors in the information below. Then type the information correctly on a postcard. Address the reverse side of the card to Mr G Forster, 33 Debden Road, Hexham, Northumberland, NE46 7XT.

```
HIE-LAND INDUSTRIES LIMITED            Telex 939203
Hie-Land House   77 Cassel Park Lane
Bridgeside  EDINBURGH  EH2 4AF      Tel 031-557 4571
```

Dateas Postmark

Thank you for your application too attend our Centen-
Centenary Celebration Open Day. we pologise for this
formal methodof acknowledging your application, but
but we have received a unexpectedly large no of
applications. Your official invitation & further
details will be sent to you within a few a few days

Assignment 73

a. When you work in an office you should make a . . . copy of every letter you type.

b. List 5 items that are always included on a business letter.

c. What items are typed at the top of a continuation sheet to a letter?

d. A circular letter with spaces in which 'variable' or 'personalised' details can be inserted is known as a . . . or . . . letter.

e. What items may be omitted from the message side of a business postcard?

12 COLUMN LAYOUT AND TABULATION

Assignment 74

Centre the following table horizontally and vertically on the page.

HAIR CREATIONS INTERNATIONAL — DARVILLE

Open Monday to Saturday — Late Night Thursday

	Junior Designer	Designer	Advanced Designer	Stylist	Tutor
Cut and Blow	£2.95	£3.85	£4.65	£6.00	£8.25
Perms from	£6.10	£7.65	£8.95	£16.00	£17.50
Highlights	£4.75	£4.75	£5.60	£11.00	£16.70

Assignment 75

Centre the following table horizontally and vertically on the page. Ensure that the paragraph of text does not extend beyond the left and right margins of the table.

DELLAMERE SURGERY STOOL

The Dellamere Surgery Stool has been comfortable and ergonomically designed for posture correct and it incorporates a fully-adjustable backrest. The now gas-lift height adjustment is guaranteed for 2 years. Safety features include a chrome-plated 5-star base with a foot ring. The attractive upholstery is fully flame-retardant and hard-wearing.*

MODEL NUMBER	STYLE	PRICE**	MODEL
DSS/202	Without backrest	£96.00	Cherie
DSS/200	With backrest	£109.00	Caroline
kSS/001	De luxe model	£165.00	Camilla

* Colours available: Black, grey, tan, champagne and blue

** Prices shown exclude VAT

Assignment 76

Type the table shown below, following the layout indicated. Use horizontal ruling only, as shown. Type underlined items in capitals, and all other items in lower case—with initial capitals where appropriate. Use leader dots. Centre horizontally and vertically on the page.

WYNNSFORD MOTOR COMPANY LIMITED

~~XXXXXXXX~~ WYNNSFORD GARAGE

OPENING HOURS *Caps*	FROM *Caps*	TO
~~XXXXXX~~	~~AM HRS~~ Hours	~~PM HRS~~ Hours
PETROL		
Monday to Saturday	0730	2200
Sunday and Bank Holidays	0900	1700
REPAIRS AND BODY SHOP		
Monday to Friday	0830	1700
~~XXXXXXXX~~ Saturday	0900	1400
SALES AND HIRE		
Monday to Friday (Summer)	0830	2000
Monday to Friday (Winter)	0830	1900
Saturday	0900	1730
Sunday	1030	1700
PARTS DEPARTMENT		
Monday to Friday	0830	1730
Saturday	0900	1400

Assignment 77

Type the following table and rule as indicated.

STOCKLIST *sp. Caps.*

STOCK SIZES	KG PER 1,000 SHEETS		
	60 g/m²	70 g/m²	85 g/m²
SRA2 (45 x 64 cm)	17.3 kg	20.2 kg	24.5 kg
RA2 (43 cm x 61 cm)	—	18.4 kg	22.3 kg
Double Cap (43 cm x 69 cm)	17.8 kg	20.8 kg	25.2 kg
Large Post (42 cm x 53 cm)	13.4 kg	15.6 kg	18.9 kg

cm

Assignment 78

Type the following circular letter on headed paper. Do not leave space for the name/address of the addressee or the signature. Rule the table as shown. No carbon copy is required.

Dear Customer

Thank you for yr. enquiry about WUNDAWHITE boards. Our new range of white-boards offers a ~~variety~~ ~~range~~ of surfaces and features. ~~to meet your needs~~

The patented surfaces of WUNDAWHITE boards accept "wet-wipe" or "dry-wipe" markers and double as projection screens. We give below a table which shd help you to select the most appropriate board for your purposes.

BOARD	WHAT IT WILL DO	WHAT IT WILL NOT DO	PRICE*
Magawhite 6' x 4'	Dry wipe	Wet wipe Hold magnets	£110.50
Markawhite 6' x 4'	Wet wipe Hold magnets	Dry wipe	£126.75
Magnawhite 5'4" x 4' (Double-sided)	Dry wipe Hold magnets	Wet wipe Give low-glare projection	£115.50
Writewhite 6' x 4'	Wet/dry wipe Hold magnets	Give low-glare projection	£102.75

* Prices exclude VAT

All WUNDAWHITE boards are designed and made in the United Kingdom to ~~the~~ highest standards. WUNDAWHITE boards ~~for~~ are extremely light in relation to their size, which makes them easy to handle and truly portable.

NP [We enclose a copy of our latest catalogue and price list and look forward to receiving your order.

Yrs scly, Howard Thingwall Sales Manager.

Assignment 79

Type the following table. Rule as shown. Centre horizontally and vertically on the page.

COSTA BLANCA FOR A WINTER HOLIDAY

Average Temperatures & Hours of Sunshine

	OCT	NOV	DEC	JAN	FEB	MAR	APR
← TEMPERATURE							
Average maximum daytime temperature	76°F	68°F	62°F	60°F	63°F	67°F	70°F
HOURS OF SUNSHINE							
Avge maximum hours of sunshine	6.7	6.0	5.6	5.8	6.8	7.1	8.7

TYPIST Leave months abbreviated

Assignment 80

Type the following table. Rule as shown. Centre horizontally and vertically on the page.

CHARMIAN LINES — sp. Caps   Retain abbreviations

Passenger Fares

Single Fare Per Person (Excluding Meals)	Low Season		High Season	
	Weekdays Mon-Fri	Weekends Sat-Sun	Weekdays Mon-Fri	Weekends Sat-Sun
Sleeperette	£55	£65	£95	£105
4-Berth Cabin	£85	£95	£115	£125
2-Berth Cabin	£97	£107	£127	£137
De-Luxe Cabin	£127	£137	£155	£165
Stateroom	£142	£152	£166	£176

Children under 4 years free provided no separate berth required.

47

Assignment 81

Use memo-headed paper. Take 1 carbon copy. Rule the table as shown, on both the top and carbon copy. Find and correct 6 spelling errors.

FROM   Mr K G Knight   REF   KGK/TBMS *Your initials*

TO   Miss B W Wroxford   DATE

CONFERANCE FACILITIES - TREVALLAN HOTEL

As requested, I called in at the Trevallan Hotel when I visited the Norwich Offices last week and the ~~Conference~~ Manager kindly *Conference* gave me a guided tour of the Conferance facilities. The hotel *Conference* has 5 ~~meetings~~ rooms - details as below.
suitable

Room/Suite	Seating Capacity		
	Theatre Style	Banquet	Exhibition Square Meters
~~Alvareda~~ *Alvardo* Hall . . .	150	150	186
Salmeda	75	50	93
Wareham . . . *eu*	85	50	90
Lady~~ville~~ *Villenve*	60	40	82
Fermor	45	45	54
Norvena	30	12	~~41~~ 42

Although we originaly thought of using one large hall, I feel - after viewing the rooms - that our best plan would be to hire the Wareham *Villenve* and Lady~~ville~~ suites. These two rooms have sliding doors between them, and this would give us some flexability in layout of the conferance room and the exhibition materials. I enclose a leaflet *and* giving floor plans of the various rooms, ~~with~~ measurements ~~marked on the plans,~~ which you should find useful. ~~once~~ As soon as I know wether you agree with my suggestion I will let you have some provissional costings.

Assignment 82

See how quickly you can find and correct 16 errors in the following table. Then type the table correctly in double line spacing under the heading FLORA CARAVANS. Rule the table.

MODEL	LENGHT	TYPE	NUMBER OF BERTHS	FEATURES	PRICE*
Woodland Fern	22' 0"	Static Van	5 Berths	No Shower	£4,999
Moorland Heather	24'	Static Van	5 Berths	Shower	£5,245
Fenland Reed	25' 9"	Static van	6 Births	Shower	5,499
Upland Rose.........	27'9"	Static Van	8 Berths	Shower	£5,750
Highland Heatherbell	30' 0"	Static Van	9 berths	Shower	£6255
Lowland Gorse .....;	33' 9'	Static Van	10 Berth	No Show r	£6,950

*   Exclusing Vat

KEYS TO ASSIGNMENTS

Key to Test Questions in Section 1

(1) Pica type, 10 characters to 1″, known as 10 Pitch. Elite type, 12 characters to 1″, known as 12 Pitch.

(2) 6.

(3) Left—25 mm (1″); Right—13 mm (½″); Top—25 mm (1″); Bottom—25 mm (1″).

(4) Do not divide:

19,724–37,605	OXFAM	Mr G W K Wynn-Chase
1998–1999	straight	through

Divide the following words at the point shown by the oblique stroke:

once-/over	print-/out	consum/ables
para/graphs	circum/spect	pro/cessing or process/ing
through/out	work/force	com/prehensive or
		compre/hensive or
		comprehen/sive

(5) Hanging style paragraph in single line spacing.

(6) Blocked style paragraphs in 1½ line spacing.

(7) Indented paragraphs in double line spacing.

(8) A4—210 mm×297 mm; A5—210 mm×148 mm; A6—105 mm×148 mm.

(9) 500.

(10) A4 portrait—100 Elite, 82 Pica.
A5 portrait—70 Elite, 59 Pica.
A5 landscape—100 Elite, 82 Pica.

(11) A4 portrait—70.
A5 portrait—49.
A5 landscape—35.

Key to Assignment 1

Are there times when you would like to hire a video film but
are put off by the thought of having to travel to your local
video club - and of having to travel there again to return the
film? Here's your answer! The "TWO-SOME VIDEO CLUB" will
call at your home twice a week - on Tuesdays and Fridays
between 6.00 pm and 10.00 pm with a travelling video library.

If you haven't got a video recorder, you can hire one from our
parent company - "TIMES-TWO TV" - at very competitive rates.
We shall be calling on you this week to introduce our new
mobile video service.

Key to Assignment 2

Fiona McGovern is a young golfer seeking sponsorship so that she can take part in the European Ladies' Golf Tour next year. Many of her friends and colleagues feel that Miss McGovern has a good future in world class golf - but she has a problem! She is stuck in her home country of New Zealand, unable to afford the fare to the UK and the finance necessary for the tour of Europe.

TRG Management PLC are helping Miss McGovern by seeking sponsors to help pay her costs. Mr R P K Wolf-James, a director of TRG, said "Fiona is more than just a good golfer - she has world-class potential, and she has a great deal to offer sponsoring companies."

Key to Assignment 3

Mr T D Jemburn BS TD
362 Pacifico Avenue
SOUTH PASADENA   CA 9130
USA

Mr C A Yeung
Cheong Hing Co Ltd
313 Temple Road
KOWLOON
HONG KONG

Mr V A Owaleda
YGA Textile Manufacturing Co Ltd
PO Box 39
PORT OF SPAIN
TRINIDAD
West Indies

PERSONAL

Professor T Guidy PhD MICE
62a Chalk Hill Lane
WEST CROYDON
Surrey   CRO 4DF

CONFIDENTIAL

Mr G Walter O'Brannigan
92 St Jude's Avenue
BELFAST
BT7 4AQ

Alhaji J S Adejumobi
42 Central Avenue
Bodija Estate
IBADAN
NIGERIA

Miss B H Belleville-Ray
Flat 7
439 Tooramie Road
TOORAK
Victoria   3142
AUSTRALIA

Chief A S Okunle
Box 4761
Ife Road
LAGOS
NIGERIA

Key to Assignment 4

Mr E G McDevitt, Secretary of the local branch of SENCIT, described the new group as an "umbrella organisation" set up to achieve effective co-ordination of the efforts of the multifarious bodies helping senior citizens in the area.

The group is currently based at the Wigg Lane, Colbury, headquarters of the CCVS (Colbury Council for Voluntary Services). Mr McDevitt explained that the CCVS had helped to launch the SENCIT organisation in the district.

"The District Health Committee has just granted us representation on its Planning Team for the Elderly," he told us. "At present SENCIT is funded mainly by the DHSS 'Opportunities for Volunteers Fund', but this source of finance is for a limited period only, and we shall soon have to rely on our own fund-raising efforts."

The spelling errors were 'umberella' (umbrella), 'affective' (effective) and 'presant' (present).

Key to Assignment 5

Attention all householders in the Colbury district ! If you have bulky household waste (eg, scrap D.I.Y. materials, old furniture, garden rubbish) youcan take it to the to the County Council's free disposal centres at Glendale Road or Abbey Lane.

The centres are open every day of the week at the following hours: Saturday - Thursday, 9.00 am - 5.00 pm; Friday, 9.00 am - 7.00 pm (May - September); Friday, 09.00 am - 4.00 pm (October - April).

NB: The disposal centres now have facilities for re - cycling waste oil, scrap paper and scarp metal.

Attention all householders in the Colbury district! If you have
bulky household waste (eg, scrap DIY materials, old furniture,
garden rubbish) you can take it to the County Council's free
disposal centres at Glendale Road or Abbey Lane.

The centres are open every day of the week at the following hours:
Saturday - Thursday, 9.00 am - 5.00 pm; Friday, 9.00 am - 7.00 pm
(May - September); Friday, 9.00 am - 4.00 pm (October - April).

NB: The disposal centres now have facilities for re-cycling waste
oil, scrap paper and scrap metal.

Key to Assignment 6

a. Two

b. Open punctuation

c. (ii) 4.30 pm

d. (iv) 0830 hours

Key to Assignment 7

FIRST AID TRAINING COURSES

For Factory and Office

Introductory Course This course is designed to teach students
all aspects of practical First Aid, using materials provided in
First Aid Boxes. To add realism, simulated injuries are used
on the "casualties" on which the trainees practise.

Refresher Course Suitable for staff who have undertaken
initial training, but who wish to revise their skills and learn
the most up-to-date techniques.

Appointed Persons Course This course is organised to meet the
needs of small businesses, where fully-qualified First Aiders
are not required, but where a member of staff trained in
emergency procedures is needed to comply with Health and Safety
recommendations.

Key to Assignment 8

FLORABUNDA PLANT ARRANGEMENTS

SPECIALLY DESIGNED TO ENHANCE YOUR OFFICE ENVIRONMENT

FELICITY   A trough filled with a variety of silk plants
             and/or flowers in a range of sizes.

MARIANNA   A large basket arrangement of silk flowers and
             plants.

CORINNA   A large free-standing planter with a silk tree
             surrounded by green foliage plants.

ARIADNE   A cascading hanging basket filled with flowers
             and foliage to create a splash of colour for any
             ceiling/wall area.

DENISE   A pottery container filled with small silk
             plants and flowers suitable for brightening up
             the reception desk or any working area.

Key to Assignment 9

FLORABUNDA PLANT ARRANGEMENTS

A new way to decorate your office

Are you looking for something different in office decor? Then
we are sure you will be delighted with our lovely Florabunda
Plant Arrangements, designed by award-winning florists in a
wide range of colours and sizes.

      WE WILL DESIGN PLANTERS, TROUGHS, BASKETS, ETC, TO
      MATCH YOUR OFFICE DECOR OR YOUR COMPANY COLOURS AT
      NO EXTRA COST.

Florabunda arrangements are solidly set in their containers so
that they cannot be damaged in transit - or when you decide to
move them around.

      WE CAN DESIGN ARRANGEMENTS TO FIT AN EXACT SPACE, OR
      AS A SCREEN, TO MEET YOUR EXACT REQUIREMENTS AT VERY
      LITTLE EXTRA COST.

Remember - silk flowers never wilt or droop, and occasional
dusting is all the maintenance they need, so you save money in
the long term.

The spelling errors were 'florrists' (florists), 'coulors' (colours), 'occassional' (occasional) and
'maintainance' (maintenance).

Key to Assignment 10

a. Any 4 from: capitals with/without underscore, spaced capitals with/without underscore, lower case with underscore, lower case with initial capitals and underscore, bold print (emboldening).

b. 5.

c. Hanging.

d. Side.

Key to Assignment 11

```
SOUTHERN STAR HOLIDAYS

BOOKING CONDITIONS


Deposit

     A deposit of £100 per person is payable when you
confirm your reservation.

Travel Insurance

     We strongly recommend that you purchase travel
insurance at the time of booking.

Single Supplement

     A single supplement must be paid where one person is
travelling alone by choice.

Travel Documents

     You are responsible for obtaining the appropriate
visa(s).  You must carry a valid passport at all times.

Refunds

     No refund is available after the tour has commenced in
respect of any trips, accommodation or meals not taken.
```

Key to Assignment 12

```
PLANT ARRANGEMENT NAMES              PLANT ARRANGEMENT NAMES

Imogen - bamboo trough               Anastasia - tall pottery vase
Hildebrand - teared planter          Brigitta - copper jug
Phillomena - decorative wheel        Catriona - small square basket
Georgina - circular planter          Georgiana - circular planter
Anastasia - tall pottry vase         Hildebrand - tiered planter
Myfanny - large oval basket          Imogen - bamboo trough
Wilhelmena - triple candle stick     Johanna - pinewood trough
Briggitta - copper jug               Myfanwy - large oval basket
Katriona - small square basket       Philomena - decorative wheelbarrow
Joanna - pine-wood trough            Wilhelmena - triple candlestick
```

Key to Assignment 13

T E L E T E X [1]

Teletex is a speedy, relatively inexpensive, method of electronic mail communication between computers and word processors, which has many benefits.

Speed A full A4 page of text can be transmitted to its destination within a few seconds.

Efficiency Messages can be stored during the day and automatically sent out during the cheaper rate periods overnight. One document can be sent automatically to a number of recipients in different locations.

Appearance Teletex has a full range of character sets and page formats, and documents retain the appearance of a normal typewritten page. [2]

International Access Teletex is an international standard agreed through CCITT [3] and a computer in one country can communicate directly with another almost anywhere in the world.

---

(1) Sometimes called 'Super Telex'.

(2) Unlike Telex, which is restricted to capital letters and a restricted page format.

(3) International Telegraph and Telephone Consultative Committee.

Key to Assignment 14

A=J; B=D; C=G; D=H; E=B; F=I; G=C; H=E; I=F; J=A.

Key to Assignment 15

The gardens at Vergremont Castle offer a rich variety of botanical specimens and beautiful vistas. The water gardens incorporate several pools, dotted with islands, and filled with ornamental fish swimming gently among the water lilies. There is a wooded picnic area by the lake and secluded play areas for the children.

The Castle, which is the home of the present Marchioness of Vergremont, is open to the public from 1 May to 30 September.

The tea-room, sited in the old bake-house, provides home-made fare. Souvenirs may be bought in the Gift Shop, and plants are sold in the walled garden of the Castle.

The spelling errors were 'ornemental' (ornamental), 'seclueded' (secluded), 'sighted' (sited), 'souveniers' (souvenirs).

Key to Assignment 16

Plasti-Post envelopes are (much) better than ordi(nary) paper envelopes. Less weigh(t) means you pay less postage charges. (They) are easier to handle and (and) quick(er) to pack and seal. Plast(i-)Post envelopes take up only (about) a (a) quarter of the sto(re)a(g)e space of paper envelopes. In addition, Plasti-Post envelopes are (also) water-repellent and tough for (the) maximum protection.

PLASTI-POST envelopes are better than ordinary paper envelopes. Less weight means you pay less in postage charges. They are easier to handle and quicker to pack and seal. PLASTI-POST envelopes take up only a quarter of the storage space of paper envelopes. In addition, PLASTI-POST envelopes are water-repellant and tough for maximum protection.

Key to Assignment 17

SOUTH SEA ISLANDS CRUISE

Your Cruise Itinerary

SUNDAY: PAPEETE TO OPUNOHU BAY, MOOREA

The "Southern Empresse" leaves Papeete's
busy and colourful waterfront and crosses
the "Sea of the Moon" to Moorea.

MONDAY: RAIATEA TO UTUROA

Overnight the "Southern Empresse" carries
you to the island of Raiatea, fringed with
coral reefs and a blue lagoon. After a
picnic lunch on the beach, you cruise to
Uturoa, with a chance to explore this
intriguing town.

TUESDAY: UTUROA TO BORA BORA

By morning you will reach Bora Bora, and
enjoy a day's cruising in the lagoon. In
the evening you will be entertained by a
typical Tahitian dance group at a
beach-side restaurant.

WEDNESDAY: TAHA'A TO HUAHINE

Taha'a will be waiting to greet you when
you wake. The morning will be spent
cruising round the entire island with a
break for swimming and snorkelling in the
lagoon. In the late evening you reach
the lagoon of Huahine.

THURSDAY: HUAHINE TO PAPEETE

During the morning you cruise to d'Avea Bay for a lazy day swimming and
snorkelling. Lunch is an authentic Tahitian Feast prepared by a local
restaurant. The day is rounded off by the Captain's Dinner, with floral
garlands and dancing, while the ship cruises through the night to arrive
at Papeete at 8.00 am on Friday morning.

Key to Assignment 18

C O M P U S C O T I A

COMPUTER SYSTEMS AND COMMUNICATIONS CONSULTANTS

Communications Bureau

Microcomputers

Software Packages

Word Processing Systems

Prestel

Telex

Teletex

130-132 PERIVALE BOULEVARD
GLASGOW
G2 4RR

Key to Assignment 19

HILVERDALE PRACTICE AIDS

for surgery, office and reception

Practice Account Book - Loose-Leaf Sheets	
Income and Expenditure	25 Sheets
Analysis	25 Sheets
Petty Cash and Wages	30 Sheets
Daily Takings Sheet	100-Sheet Pad
Schedule Error Sheets	50-Sheet Pad
General Anaesthetic Advice Cards	500 Cards
Receipt Book	Minimum 25 Books
Altered Appointment Card	500 Cards, Unheaded
Peelable Sterilizer Pouches	Reel of 250
Waste Disposal Bags	Box of 250
X-Ray Peel-Off Window Mount	Packet of 100
X-Ray Mounting Strip	250 Pre-Cut Strips

Key to Assignment 20

L I N G U A - S O F T

from

JEMMISON AUTOMATION

Jemmison Automation are the leading suppliers of integrated business software for microcomputers written in several European languages. Our software is designed to meet the needs of users all over the world, wherever these languages are spoken.

AVAILABLE IN

ENGLISH

FRENCH

GERMAN

DUTCH

SPANISH

PORTUGUESE

ITALIAN

We can also supply software in "American English" with American spellings and terminology. Our brochure gives full details, and callers are welcome to examine - and try out - our full range of microcomputer software.

THOUSANDS OF USERS WORLD-WIDE

Key to Assignment 21

FENSOME 'UPLIGHTERS'
FOR
INDIRECT LIGHTING IN YOUR OFFICE

Do your staff suffer from eyestrain, headaches and glare? Are you using too much energy through an inefficient lighting system? Indirect lighting from FENSOME UPLIGHTERS offers:

Elegant designs
Modern colour range
Simple re-location
Minimum standing space
Low installation costs
Low maintenance costs

The errors were: sufffer (suffer), throuhg (through), lightning (lighting), form (from), elegent (elegant), color (colour), Minimun (Minimum), installaton (installation), Lowe (Low) and maintainance (maintenance).

Key to Assignment 22

T R E N D   A N D   T R I M M E R   L I M I T E D

proudly announce their appointment as

SPECIALIST FLEET CAR DEALER FOR GRIFFON CARS

Our expertise in handling fleet operations, both large and small, enables us to meet your needs precisely.

THE NORTH'S LEADING FLEET SPECIALISTS

This specialised knowledge of day-to-day and long-term business requirements has been built up over years of experience and is now endorsed by Griffon Cars themselves with this new appointment.

LET US GIVE YOU A QUOTATION

We can meet your company's needs - whether you want just a few cars or a fleet of hundreds. Our specialists will deal with your fleet enquiries and tell you about the outstanding quality and unbeatable prices we offer.

NEW CONTRACT HIRE AND LEASING SERVICE

The errors were CAR'S (CARS), NORTHS' (NORTH'S), year's (years), companys (company's), need's (needs), specialist's (specialists) and enquiry's (enquiries).

Key to Assignment 23

TREND & TRIMMER LIMITED

THE NORTH'S LEADING FLEET SERVICE

Contact our Specialist Staff

for any

Fleet Enquiries on 061-222 76770

Daniel Ireland	General Sales Manager
William Preece-Jones	Fleet Sales Manager
Fenjal Supri	Sales Executive
Louis Basque	Local Fleet Specialist
Samantha Hoosemain	Fleet Sales Controller
Alex Brittain	Fleet Service Specialist

Key to Assignment 24

M E M O R A N D U M

FROM   Miss Heidi Clare   REF   HC/your initials
       Word Processing Centre

TO   Mrs Vera Landon   DATE (Today's date)
       Office Services Manager

NEW COPYHOLDERS

Now that we have converted the Centralised Typing Section to the Word
Processing Centre, the existing copyholders which were used by staff in
the typing pool for several years, are proving unsatisfactory for the
word processing operators.   I have received a number of complaints from
operators of the awkward angle at which the copy must be placed with
these copyholders, resulting (they claim) in neck-ache, eyestrain and
fatigue.

I enclose a brochure giving details of electrically-operated copyholders
designed specially for use with VDUs.

If you agree to the purchase of these new copyholders, I should like to
try out the following versions before a purchase is made, to see which
type is most satisfactory: the table-top, the spring-arm and the clamp
version.

Will you please let me know as soon as possible if you are able to
arrange this.

Key to Assignment 25

M E M O R A N D U M

FROM   Cedric Farrier   REF   CF/your initials
       Sports and Social Club

TO   All Members of Staff   DATE (Today's date)

DOG TRAINING CLASSES

Is your puppy driving you up the wall? Would you like to improve
your dog's behaviour? Do you have a "problem pet"? Are you
willing to learn and improve your ability as a dog handler?

The Sports and Social Club has arranged a series of Dog Training
Classes, to be held on Saturday mornings from 10.00 am to 11.30 am.

Interested? Want further details? Contact Philip Mexborough on
Ext 242 as soon as possible.

Key to Assignment 26

M E M O R A N D U M

FROM	John P Childers Personnel Manager	REF	JPC/your initials
TO	Sara Meacham Training Department	DATE	(Today's date)

FIRST AID TRAINING

As you are aware, the Health and Safety Executive has set up strict requirements for ensuring adequate levels of proficiency for First Aiders in offices and work-places. During the past year there have been several occasions when we have encountered difficulties in providing the correct level of cover, particularly during the summer holiday period.

Will you please arrange for a series of Training Sessions for First Aiders. We urgently need a course for new First Aiders. In addition we require some refresher classes for people who have undertaken training in their previous employment but who have not taken up the role of First Aider with our company. Mr Ashuola has agreed that, if necessary, you may use the services of a commercial training company. Let me have details as soon as possible.

The grammatical errors were: there has been (there have been); need urgently (urgently need); refresher class (refresher classes); of commercial (a commercial).

Key to Assignment 27

a. A formal beginning, such as 'Dear Mr Jones', and a formal ending, such as 'Yours faithfully'.

b. To indicate that something has been enclosed with the memo.

c. The origin of the memo, eg, the name/designation and/or department of the sender; the name(s) of the recipients; the date.

d. The name and/or designation/department of the recipient; the date; the page number.

e. The originator's reference; the subject heading; courtesy titles; distribution details; enclosure notation.

Key to Assignment 28

Memos may be typed on (on) pre-printed memo-headed paper or on (on) plain paper, depending on (on) the practice of the (the) company in which you work. (work.) Remember that you are (you are) always expected to insert the date, (the date,) even if you are not given instructions to do (to do) so. You should also insert an (insert an) appropriate reference, even if you are (you are) not told to do so. Always proofread your work and ensure that it (it) is accurate before you return it to (it to) the author for (for) signature.

Key to Assignment 29

M E M O R A N D U M

FROM   Mr G D Darling   REF   GDD/your initials
        Maintenance Department

TO   All Heads of Department   DATE   (Today's date)

SAFETY OF ELECTRIC PLUGS

As requested by the Health and Safety Committee, I have conducted a
thorough survey of the condition of electric plugs in the company's
offices. A full report has been prepared for the Health and Safety
Committee, but a summary of findings is given below for your
information.

CONDITION OF PLUG CASING

Each plug case was inspected for chips or cracks and missing screws,
and 5.6% of the plugs had serious physical damage. Some of these
were dangerous - one, in fact, was broken in half and was held
together by clear adhesive cellulose tape.

INCORRECT WIRING

Each plug was inspected for incorrect wiring, and about 1.2% were
faulty, mainly due to the reversal of positive and negative wires.

CONDITION OF CORD GRIP

The plugs were checked for condition of the cord grip, and 20% were
found to be faulty. The main problems arose from missing/loose
screws, and in some cases the cord grip was not in use at all.

UNSATISFACTORY FUSES

Most plugs were fitted with a 13 amp fuse, irrespective of the
rating of the appliance being used. It was found that 86% of the
plugs were fitted with a 13 amp fuse when a lower rated fuse should
be employed.

GENERAL CONCLUSIONS

The highest proportion of faults was found on "unauthorised"
equipment such as private kettles and coffee-making machines.

It is clear that the condition of electric plugs throughout the
company's offices is most unsatisfactory, and that as all plugs are
inspected and checked when equipment is installed, it is clear that
members of staff are "tampering" with them at a later stage.

TO   All Heads of Department   -2-   DATE   (Today's date)

RECOMMENDATIONS

(1)   A regular check should be instituted.

(2)   A clear policy that plugs and fuses are fitted and replaced
      only by maintenance staff, should be set up and adhered to.

(3)   "Unauthorised/private" appliances such as kettles, should be
      removed from all departments, and should not be replaced in
      future.

(4)   All faulty plugs should be replaced immediately.   (This is, in
      fact, already under way.)

Key to Assignment 30

It is not always necessary to include the courtesy title of the people
sending and / or receiving a memo. Some companys always use the
courtesy titles. Others have a more informal approach and memos may be
sent, forexample, from "Fred Bolder" to "Josie Kane." Other people like
to use the courtesy title for the recipient, but put there own name
without one, e g, from "Don Pierce" to "Mr G W Heron". When you work
in an office, follow the style used in your own Company

COURTESY TITLES IN MEMOS

It is not always necessary to include the courtesy title of the people
sending and/or receiving a memo. Some companies always use the
courtesy titles. Others have a more informal approach and memos may be
sent, for example, from "Fred Bolder" to "Josie Kane". Other people
like to use the courtesy title for the recipient, but put their own
name without one, eg, from "Don Pierce" to "Mr G W Heron". When you
work in an office, follow the style used in your own company.

Key to Assignment 31

SOUTHERN REGION COMMERCE & INDUSTRY EXHIBITION

Here's what some of our exhibitors said about last year's Commerce and Industry Exhibition.

"A successful and well-organised exhibition which provided a perfect opportunity to meet local companies. We'll be back next year! CROSBIE COMPUTER SYSTEMS"

"This was the second time we participated. We doubled our stand space but found the increased expenditure was well repaid because it enabled us to speak to many more members of the business community. Chris Kerrie, Senior Information Officer, FDRC LIMITED"

"The exhibition provided an excellent number of quality leads. Many of these valuable leads have been successfully followed up and resulted in further business. SOUTHERN PERSONNEL & MANAGEMENT SERVICES LIMITED"

"An unqualified success! The exhibition provided us with a very high level of contacts and we immediately re-booked for next year with a much bigger stand. William Laughton, Regional Sales Executive, DRAGOVEND LIMITED"

THE EXHIBITION WILL BE GIVEN MAXIMUM PUBLICITY
THROUGHOUT THE UNITED KINGDOM AND OVERSEAS

The errors in punctuation were: Heres (Here's), participated (participated.), more; (more), LIMITED (LIMITED"), "The (The), Laughton (Laughton,).

Key to Assignment 32

a. No carbon required.

b. Distribution.

c. Underline or tick the name of the person who is to receive the copy, using a coloured pen.

d. Blind carbon copy. Used where the sender does not wish the person receiving the top copy to know that someone else has received a copy—or where they do not feel it is necessary for the sender to know that information.

e. By writing 'File' or 'F' in the top right-hand corner of the file copy. In addition, coloured paper may be used for the file copy as an aid to identification.

f. In a noticeable position, eg, within the top margin at the right-hand side or at the bottom of the page at the right-hand side.

Key to Assignment 33

M E M O R A N D U M

FROM   Miss B Zachara   REF   BZ/your initials
       Personnel Department

TO   Mrs S A Hamad   DATE   (Today's date)
       Editor, "Boden News"

COPY TO Mr Clark Boden, Managing Director
         Mr Bernard Boden

<u>ITEM FOR "BODEN NEWS"</u>

Please ensure that the following item appears in the next issue of the
"Boden News".

"Mr Bernard Boden has now joined the company and will work his way through
the firm, department by department, gaining valuable practical experience
after his years of academic study.

"Like his father and his brother, Glen, Bernard was educated at Norgate
College, Clifton, before gaining a BSc Honours degree in Accountancy and
Managerial Studies at University College, Cardiff."

Key to Assignment 34

Walker Baby Equipment Limited warrantees that if any defect in material
or work appears in the product within a year after the date of date of
purchase, it will repair or replace the product free of charge. This
applies only if the product has been used only for domestic purposes
and has been damaged though mis-use, accident or neglect, and has
not been modified or repaired by any one other than Walker Baby
Equipment Company Limited. This is in addition to the consumers'
statutory rights and does not effect those rights in anyway.

WALKER BABY EQUIPMENT LIMITED

Walker Baby Equipment Limited warrants that if any defect in materials

or workmanship appears in the product within one year after the date of

purchase, it will repair or replace the product free of charge. This

applies only if the product has been used solely for domestic purposes

and has not been damaged through misuse, accident or neglect, and has

not been modified or repaired by anyone other than Walker Baby

Equipment Limited. This warranty is in addition to the consumer's

statutory rights and does not affect those rights in any way.

Key to Assignment 35

M E M O R A N D U M

FROM   Mr P D Pendry   REF   PDP/your initials
       Research Department

TO   Mr A G Farsi   DATE   (Today's date)
       Technical Director

NEW MULTI-PURPOSE SCOPES

In answer to the queries raised in your memo, Miss Grey has provided the following information.

A specially-designed programmable interface for the instrument controllers ensures that measurement results are captured from the instrument for processing and analysis by the controller. Accurate voltage and current measurements are made using crosshair cursors.

A window mode displays minimum and maximum test limits in "GO/NO-GO" testing procedures. A sequencing mode automatically steps through a series of test cycles without the help of a controller. Devices may also be cycled through tests automatically under program control.

Key to Assignment 36

M E M O R A N D U M

FROM   Mr G A Woodhead   REF   GAW/your initials
       Managing Director

TO   Mr H Kemp   DATE   (Today's date)
       Public Relations Manager

HEMMANFORD AGRICULTURAL SHOW

As discussed with you, the Board was very disappointed with the quality of the company's stand and marquee at the Hemmanford Show last week. The poor weather added to the difficulties, of course, but it is obvious that we need an alternative to the marquee for next year's show.

A friend of mine mentioned that Fleetgood Caravans in Abberley hire out prestige caravan units for use as 'hospitality suites' at shows of this kind. I understand they are supplied complete with integral kitchen, bar and seating area. If necessary, a generator can also be hired.

Please contact Fleetgood and let me have your opinions on the suitability of one, or perhaps two, of these caravans for our purposes. It might be an idea to try out one of the units at the Foreham Flower Show as an experiment. Have a look at the caravans personally and let me know what the costs would be, as soon as possible.

Key to Assignment 37

BATIKA ALUMINIUM GREENHOUSES

1   Generous 4' 9" eaves height (9" higher than any of our competitors' makes).

2   Straight sides to give more room for tall plants.

3   All glass is 24 oz (3 mm) thick, horticultural grade, 24" x 24".

4   Built-in 2½" guttering and condensation channels along the two longer sides.

5   Standard sizes: 6' 2" x 6' 2"; 6' 2" x 8' 0"; 6' 2" x 10' 2½"; 6' 2" x 12' 3"; 6' 2" x 14' 3½" and 6' 2" x 16' 0" long.

6   Free staging for all 6' 2" x 16' 0" greenhouses.

7   Roof-opening ventilators can be positioned wherever desired along the ridge bar. One window is provided for 6' 2" - 8' 0" sizes, two windows for 10' 2½" - 12' 3" sizes and four windows for 14' 3½" - 16' 0" sizes.

The inconsistencies were: 24 inch×24"; 2½ inch; 6' 2" by 16' 0"; 6' 2"−8'; 4 windows; 14' 3½"−16 ft sizes.

Key to Assignment 38

IMPROVING EFFICIENCY

1   NEED FOR TRAINING

A recent survey claimed that over 80% of microcomputer users could gain more benefit from their computer. Three areas were highlighted:

      1.1   More training by experienced and qualified staff.
      1.2   Better training, more specifically related to company needs.
      1.3   Increased practice time following training courses.

2   MAJOR USES

The survey revealed the four major uses of executive microcomputers, as listed below:

      2.1   Perhaps surprisingly, the major use was for spreadsheets and financial applications.
      2.2   Word processing was the next highest use.
      2.3   Database management was widely used.
      2.4   Relatively few users made extensive use of graphics programs.

Key to Assignment 39

KIRKWARDLE AT BARFIELD HIRING FAIR AGAIN

For the fifth time our Barfield Depot provided temporary floodlighting for the Barfield Hiring Fair so that visitors would be
sure to see all the highlights of this popular event.

A total of 32 Mobile 'Towerlights', each 21.35 m high, were
strategically positioned to assist in security operations and to
illuminate car park entries and walkways throughout the Fair site.

Five of our engineers were stationed on the site throughout the 4
days of the Fair to oversee the delivery and erection of the
'Towerlights' and provide a full maintenance service.

> Barfield Hiring Fair was first held in 1284 under a
> right conferred by Edward I. The principal activity
> in those days was the hiring of agricultural and
> domestic labour, together with the sale of poultry
> and vegetable produce.
>
> The Fair moved to its present site at Garston Park,
> 3.2 km from the city centre, in 1932. Today's
> Hiring Fair provides dozens of modern fairground
> rides, plus 100-150 sideshows and stalls for the
> 500,000 or more people who visit the Fair every
> year.

In the past 2 years we have also been asked to provide temporary
office accommodation and mobile toilets for the administration
centre. These consisted of 2 portable units 9.75 m x 3.05 m for
use by First Aid staff, and a 7.35 m x 2.75 m office used by the
organisers as a retrieval point for lost children. We also
supplied 4 of our 5.80 m main toilet units for use by the many
thousands of people who visited the Fair.

Key to Assignment 40

<u>SPECIFICATION</u>

Machine deckle: 6,600 mm
Grammage range: 60 g/m² to 135 g/m²
Reel widths: min 200 mm, max 2,400 mm
Reel diameters: 800 mm and 1,000 mm
Boxes per pallet: 40 (500 kg) and 80 (1,000 kg)
Reams per box: A4 - 5 or 10
Wrapping: White 90 g/m² bleached kraft

<u>SPECIFICATION</u>

Machine deckled: 6,600 mm
Grammage range; 60 g/m³ to 135 g/m²
Reel widths: min 20 mm, max 2,400 mm
Reel diameters: 800 mm and 1000 mm
Boxed per pallett) 40 (500 kg and 80 (1,000 kg)
Reams per box: A5 - 5 (kg) or 10 (kg)
Wrapping) White 90 g/m bleached kraft

<u>SPECIFICATION</u>

Boxes per pallet: 40 (500 kg) and 80 (1,000 kg)

Grammage range: 60 g/m² to 135 g/m²

Machine deckle: 6,600 mm

Reams per box: A4 - 5 or 10

Reel widths: min 200 mm, max 2,400 mm

Reel diameters: 800 mm and 1,000 mm

Wrapping: White 90 g/m² bleached kraft

Key to Assignment 41

M E M O R A N D U M

FROM   John Danvers   REF   JD/your initials

TO   Alex Cinnamond   DATE   (Today's date)

Will you please arrange for the following advertisement to be placed
in the next issue of "Industrial Property Monthly".

HOLT-HIGHLANDS PROPERTY

COMMERCIAL DEPARTMENT

(a) PAISLEY   Nantfield Lane. Warehouse and offices - 48,000 sq ft.
                Site area 1.55 acres. £275,000 subject to contract.

(b) RENFREW   Corby Road Industrial Estate. Newly-built
                warehouse/industrial units on established estate.
                Steel Portal Frame 16 ft 6 in eaves. A variety of
                units to let - 4,000 sq ft, 5,400 sq ft, 6,750 sq ft or
                14,800 sq ft. From £8.50/sq ft.

(c) GLASGOW   Hamish Street. Warehouse and offices, 67,000 sq ft,
                with car park for over 200 cars. Site area 2 acres.
                £295,000 subject to contract.

Key to Assignment 42

a. 8.

b. Two or three, consistently.

c. Above.

d. Below.

e. Litre and tonne.

f. Decimal.

Key to Assignment 43

MEXILANA OPTICAL DISK DRIVE

PHYSICAL SPECIFICATIONS

Environmental Limits

Ambient temperature: 50 $^{\circ}$F to 109 $^{\circ}$F (10 $^{\circ}$C to 43 $^{\circ}$C).

Relative humidity: 10% to 90%.

Maximum wet bulb: 80 $^{\circ}$F (26.7 $^{\circ}$C).

DC Voltage Requirements

+15 V DC ±5% @ 4 A peak.

−15 V DC ±5% @ 4 A peak.

+5 V DC ±5% @ 14 A peak.

Error Rates

Non−recoverable errors: 1 per 10^{12} bits read.

Non−detected errors: 1 per 10^{16} bits read.

Seek errors: 1 per 10^{6} seeks.

Dimensions

Height: 6.81" (173.0 mm).

Width: 17.6" (447.0 mm).

Depth: 24" (609.6 mm).

Weight: 50 lb (27.7 kg).

Key to Assignment 44

AUSTRALIAN SAFARI TREKS BY MOTOR CARAVAN

Try a Safari Trek holiday across Australia by motor caravan.
Nothing you have ever done before will compare with this holiday
of a lifetime!

(i)   The Southern Fringe Route crosses Australia between Perth
and Sydney (3,961 km/1,745 miles). The cost per person is
A$795.00.

(ii)   The Traveller Route runs between Adelaide and Perth, across
the Nullarbor Plain (2,663 km/1,664 miles) for A$620.25 per
person.

(iii)   The Springs Route between Sydney and Alice Springs
(2,857 km/1,786 miles) costs A$620.25 per person.

(iv)   The Trans-Australia makes the journey between Brisbane and
Cairns (1,681 km/1,050 miles) for only A$495.50 per person.

(v)   The Adelaide-Alice Route runs from Adelaide to Alice
Springs (1,553 km/971 miles). The cost per person is
A$395.80.

Key to Assignments 45 and 46

FLYTEPARK PARK-AND-RIDE AIRPORT SERVICE

Please reserve car parking and transport to/from airport.

Name .... Brian .... Surname .. Mackenzie ....

Address .... 402 Glasberrie Road ....

.... Port Talbot ....

Postcode .. SA12 4JB .... Telephone 06396-44217 ....

Make of Car Vauxhall .... Model ...... Astra 1300S ....

Colour .... Red .... Registration .. C 746 HRG ....

Date Outward 16 July .... Destination .. Boston, USA ....

Time of Flight 1630 hours .... Flight Number .. BA 275 ....

Date of Return 30 July .... Returning From Boston, USA ....

Flight Arrival Time 0810 hours .... Flight Number .. BA 274 ....

Number of Adults .... 2 .... Number of Children 3 ....

Number of Days ..... 14 .... Indoor/ØUXØØØX Parking*

Signed .... Date (Today's date) ....

Please arrive at Flyte House 2 hours before flight time.

* Please delete as appropriate.

Key to Assignments 47 and 48

<u>INSTITUTE OF CRAFT TECHNICIANS - ANNUAL CONFERENCE</u>

"UNUSUAL OBJECT" COMPETITION

You are invited to display an "unusual object" on the competition table during the Conference from 1600 hours on Friday, 14 April, to 1300 hours on Saturday, 15 April. You may display as many objects as you wish, but each object must be entered on a separate entry form.*

Mr Andrew Currie and Mr Leon Vila, members of the North-East Regional Committee, will judge the competition, and the person judged to have entered the most unusual object will be presented with a matched set of Darley suitcases. The result of the competition will be announced at the Dinner Dance on Saturday evening, when the winner will be expected to explain what the object is.

*   Please note that, although every effort will be made to safeguard exhibits, objects are displayed at the owner's risk and no responsibility can be accepted for loss or breakage.

- -

E N T R Y   F O R M

"UNUSUAL OBJECT" COMPETITION

Name .... Jennifer Holmeswood ....

Address .... 39 Silver Bay Road, Cockermouth ....

.... Cumbria, CA13 9TQ ....

Region .... North-West .... Membership Number .... 431699 ....

BRIEF DESCRIPTION OF THE OBJECT
A small bundle of 6 irregularly-shaped wooden sticks, each stick about 14 mm long by 10 mm wide, flat on one side and roughly shaped on the other, the bundle secured by 'raffia' string.

The spelling errors were: conferance (conference), seperate (separate), safegaurd (safeguard), exibits (exhibits), responsability (responsibility), discription (description).

Key to Assignments 49 and 50

ROAD-READY AUTO SERVICE CENTRE LIMITED
12a Cross Anchor Street
GALASHIELS
TD1 7EX

Telephone: 0896-3377661

VAT Registration Number 414 7677 310

I N V O I C E

Customer <u>Mrs G Ardrossan</u>   Date <u>(Today's date)</u>

Address <u>3 Valley Road</u>   Invoice Number <u>7764</u>

<u>Galashiels</u>   Vehicle <u>Talbot Horizon</u>

_____   Registration Number <u>B 416 AGR</u>

REPAIRS	TOTAL
	£
To replacing offside brake pipe, nearside front side-light bulb, offside rear brake light bulb, releasing handbrake and blowing out rear drums and brake shoes.	
Materials - Copper Brake Pipe	4.25
Brake Fluid	2.50
2 Light Bulbs @ 0.55	1.10
2 Unions @ 0.75	1.50
Carrying out MOT Test	10.00
Labour - 2½ hours	23.75
TOTAL	43.10
PLUS VAT	6.47
TOTAL DUE	49.57

Key to Assignment 51

```
                RESERVATION POST CARD REQUEST


    Please reserve the following accommodation:

    Single Room/Double Room/Studio Suite/Suite* for

    ...... nights from ............ to ............

    I will be arriving before/after 6.00 pm*

    Signed .......................................

    *  Delete item(s) not applicable



    THIS REQUEST DOES NOT GUARANTEE A ROOM UNLESS
    CONFIRMATION IS GIVEN BY THE HOTEL IN WRITING
```

```
                                              FREEPOST




          The Primavera House Hotel
          FREEPOST
          Regents Park
          LONDON
          NW1 4JK
```

Key to Assignment 52

```
Please send me OFFICE EQUIPEMENT LISTING FREE EACH Month

Name ......................... Job tittle .................

Company name ............. ,, ............................

Buisness address ....................................

.............................. Postcode ...................

My company ' s line off business ........................

number of employees .................................

Singed ...................... date ....................
```

```
Please send me OFFICE EQUIPMENT LISTING FREE EACH MONTH

Name ......................... Job title .................

Company name ....................................

Business address ....................................

.............................. Postcode ...................

My company's line of business ........................

Number of employees .................................

Signed ...................... Date ....................
```

Did you remember to type the address on the reverse side of the card?

Key to Assignment 53

a. Double or 1½ line spacing.

b. Spaced hyphens.

c. From edge to edge of the paper. (If you use a word processor, you will probably only be able to type the line from margin to margin.)

d. At least 38 mm (1½″).

e. At least 38 mm (1½″) for a date and 32 mm (1¼″) for a telephone number.

f. Full stop or the underscore.

Key to Assignment 54

M E M O R A N D U M

FROM   Mr L G Brendan   REF   LGB/your initials
        Engineering Department

TO   All Gardening Section Members   DATE   (Today's date)
        Staff Sports and Social Club

VISIT TO MEOLSFORD HALL GARDENS

I have organised an evening excursion to Meolsford Hall Gardens on
29 June. This visit will include a guided tour round the gardens by
Lord Meolsford himself, and a light buffet meal in the Conservatory at
the end of the tour.

The cost of the excursion is £7.50, including the coach fare. The
pick-up point for the coach is the Drinkwater Hotel on Goode Street.
Only 28 places are available, and places will be allocated on a
'first-come-first-served' basis.

Please complete the reply slip below, and return it to me as soon as
possible.

- -

To Mr L G Brendan, Engineering Department

VISIT TO MEOLSFORD HALL GARDENS

Please reserve a place for me on the excursion to Meolsford Hall
Gardens on 29 June.

I enclose a cheque for £7.50.

Name _____

Department _____ Tel Extn _____

Key to Assignment 55

M E M O R A N D U M

FROM   Arnold Garthwaite   REF   AG/your initials
       Managing Director

TO   All Members of Technical Staff DATE   (Today's date)

WASTE METAL RETRIEVAL

It is essential that ALL forms of waste material that may contain
precious metals /lemel, grindings, bench sweepings, floor sweepings,
dust from extractor bags and face masks/ should be collected at the
end of each day's work and placed in the blue collection bin /but
please ensure that the bin contains a liner before depositing the
waste/.

Failure to carry out this routine is regarded as a serious disciplinary matter /as agreed with the Union Representatives (see
Section VI of Conditions of Service)/.

At the end of each month, 25% of the payment received for waste
metal will be distributed to technical staff /with deductions for
days of absence (see Section IX of Conditions of Service) excluding
holiday entitlement/.

- -

RETURN THIS SLIP TO MR A GARTHWAITE IMMEDIATELY AS A CONFIRMATION
OF RECEIPT

GRAPPENLINK LABORATORIES

WASTE METAL RETRIEVAL NOTICE

I confirm receipt of the WASTE METAL RETRIEVAL NOTICE issued on

....

Name ....

Employee Number ....

Section ....

Signature .... Date ....

Key to Assignment 56

BATAKA DESIGNER COLLECTION

RETAIL PRICE LIST

```
LONG RED CALFSKIN JACKET
Available in S, M, L, XL, XXL ................... £475.00

SHORT RED CALFSKIN JACKET
Available in S, M, L, XL ...................... £422.50

SHORT GREY CALFSKIN JACKET
Available in S, M, L, XL ...................... £422.50

GREY CALFSKIN GILET
Available in S, M, L, XL ...................... £285.75

GREY/BEIGE MOHAIR PULLOVER
Available in S, M, L, XL ...................... £75.00

DESIGNER JOGGING SUIT
Available in XS, S, M, L, XL ................... £128.80

BATAKA LEATHER BELT
Available in Red/Beige or Sand/Beige ............ £19.75
```

PRICES INCLUDE VAT

Key to Assignment 57

FREE 15-MONTH WALL PLANNING CHART.

Just in case the words "free offer" arouse your suspicions, let me assure you . . . there are no strings attached! We want to help you make your office more efficient . . . with our compliments.

The wall planning chart covers a 15-month period and has a "write-on/wipe-off" surface . . . it is invaluable for planning future activities.

If you would like one of these helpful wall planners simply post the reply card today . . . it will be my pleasure to arrange for you to receive one with our compliments.* It's ideal as a display diary . . . to plan job schedules . . . or to keep track of staff holidays.

* To be sure of receiving your free wall planning chart, please post the reply card before the end of February . . . we shall be unable to supply charts after this "closing date".

The spelling errors were: their (there); attatched (attached); recieve (receive); shedules (schedules); Febuary (February).

Key to Assignment 58

ROBO-WRITER USER MANUAL

C O N T E N T S

Key to Assignment 59

```
GOURMET BUFFET MENU

La Soupe de Crème Colombine
Les Bouchées de Champignons
La Tranche de Poissons Fumées
Le Poulet de Grain en Gelee
Le Carré de Porc sous Cruste
Fraises A la Crème
Zabaglione aux Pêaches
Les Gâteaux est Patisseries
Café et les Petits Fours

Chief: François Maçon
```

```
GOURMET BUFFET MENU

La Soupe de Crème Colombine

Les Bouchées de Champignons

La Tranche de Poissons Fumés

Le Poulet de Grain en Gelée

Le Carré de Porc sous Croûte

***

Fraises a la Crème

Zabaglione aux Pêches

Les Gâteaux et Patisseries

***

Café et les Petits Fours

*****
***


Chef: François Maçon
```

Key to Assignment 60

THE GOLDEN CUPRESSUS RESTAURANT

W I N E   L I S T

BORDEAUX

Château la Louvière £9.25
Médoc £7.25

LOIRE

Saumur Cuvée des Plantagenets £6.49
Muscadet, Château de la Galissonnière £6.65
Muscadet de Sèvre-et-Maine £6.35
Anjou Rosé £6.15

RHÔNE

Côtes du Rhône £6.15
Châteauneuf-du-Pape Domaine de Cabrières £9.45

RHINE

Bereich Schloss Böckelheim £6.25
Rüdesheimer Rosengarten £6.45
Oppenheimer Krötenbrunnen £6.15

SPAIN

Viña Esmerelda £7.25
Viña Herminia £6.55

Key to Assignment 61

GRAPPENLINK LABORATORIES

OUR SECTION STAFF - HERE TO HELP YOU!

```
Simon Knowles )
Herb Poole   )   CROWN AND BRIDGE
Oscar Schell )
Kelly Stavros)

Dandy Bevin  )
Emrys Hughes )   FULLS
Fran Wells   )
Anna Wong    )

Tod Basharu  )
Greg Likert  )   ORTHODONTICS
Pat Mackay   )
Lou Previn   )

Allen Green  )
Rudi Olawaru )   PARTIALS
Alex Timpson )

Mick Deal    )
Dan Post     )   PORCELAIN
Sandy Singh  )
Chris Youds  )

Sue Cryer    )
Rick Dover   )   REPAIRS
Marie Howe   )
Lal Patel    )
```

Key to Assignment 62

a. As continuous dots, or in groups of 5, eg, 2 dots and 3 spaces, 3 dots and 2 spaces, or 1 dot and 4 spaces.

b. To represent the word 'ditto'. To indicate that an item is repeated in a list.

c. Three spaced or unspaced full stops, used consistently.

d. Writing them in neatly with a matching colour pen.

e. By typing a set of brackets aligned under each other in single line spacing.

Key to Assignment 63

THE BEST OF OUR SUMMER WINE

We attach our latest wine list . . . a simple guide to our wide and
varied selection of wines from the best wine-producing countries in the
world.

Loire	)		Australia
Rhône	)		Austria
Alsace	)		Bulgaria
Beaujolais	)		California
Burgundy	)	France	Chile
Mâconnais-Chalonnais	)		Greece
Chablis	)		Hungary
Côte d'Or	)		Italy
Bordeaux	)		Lebanon
			Portugal
Rhine	)		Spain
Moselle	)	Germany	Yugoslavia

If you have any problems or queries, simply contact our helpful staff
in your local Cadillo wine shop . . . they are always ready to give you
the benefit of their knowledge and experience. Services provided in our
650 shops in towns and cities across the country include:

Fully-trained staff	Specialist advice
Sale or return facilities	Full party service
Free glass loan scheme	Free local deliveries
Generous quantity discounts	Wine tasting evenings

All prices include VAT at 15% and are correct as at (today's date), but
we reserve the right to change them without notice. Customers ordering a
case of 12 bottles of wine (which may be in mixed cases) are entitled to
a discount of 5% off shelf prices . . . provided the wine is not on a
special promotional offer.

Key to Assignment 64

HIE-LAND INDUSTRIES LIMITED

Hie-Land House   Telex 939203
77 Cassel Park Lane
Bridgeside   VAT Reg No 414 7677 37
EDINBURGH
EH2 4AF   Telephone 031-557 4571

```
(Today's date)


Mr H W Yarrow
Advertising Manager
Purple Thistle Radio PLC
PO Box 276
Carrick Street
EDINBURGH
EH2 4BB


Dear Mr Yarrow

Thank you for your help with our first advertising campaign with Purple
Thistle Radio, which has proved very successful.  The response to our
introductory offer from small companies in the region has been tremendous,
and this has opened up a new market for our loading equipment.

We hope to run a similar campaign towards the end of the year - when we
have re-organised our Production Department to cope with the increase in
orders.

Yours sincerely
```

Key to Assignment 65

HIE-LAND INDUSTRIES LIMITED

Hie-Land House
77 Cassel Park Lane
Bridgeside
EDINBURGH
EH2 4AF

Telex 939203

VAT Reg No 414 7677 37

Telephone 031-557 4571

Our ref GO'C/CHGF/47/17B/your initials

(Today's date)

Mr P Vegas
Group Hire Manager
Stackington-Price Ltd
7-9 Gooch Road
BATHGATE
EH48 1TS

Dear Mr Vegas

I write to thank you and everyone else involved at Stackington-Price Ltd
for the first-class service provided at the Highland Games Festival held
by our company last month to celebrate our Centenary.

The whole event went off with scarcely a hitch, and your staff are to be
congratulated for this fine achievement, and for the friendly and very
efficient manner in which they carried out their work. For your interest
I enclose a copy of our House Magazine, which contains a 10-page "spread"
on the Games.

You can be sure that we shall recommend your services to any colleagues
who are planning an event of this kind.

Yours sincerely
HIE-LAND INDUSTRIES LIMITED

Gordon O'Connell
PUBLIC RELATIONS MANAGER

Enc

Key to Assignment 66

HIE-LAND INDUSTRIES LIMITED

Hie-Land House
77 Cassel Park Lane
Bridgeside
EDINBURGH
EH2 4AF

Telex 939203

VAT Reg No 414 7677 37

Telephone 031-557 4571

Cur ref   PSB/AD/your initials

Date as Postmark

Dear Sir

Thank you for your enquiry concerning our TMG/Huger products. We have
pleasure in enclosing a copy of our booklet "Guide to Central Heating",
together with details of TMG/Huger central heating programmers, type
Hugotrol 90 and 95M.

The Hugotrol 90 is for use with gravity-fed systems, and the 95M for
installations where motorised valves are to be controlled.

At the back of the booklet is a £10 voucher, redeemable from any
distributor of Hie-Land central heating products.

For your convenience we also enclose a list of distributors. However, if
you have any difficulty in obtaining TMG/Huger equipment, we shall be
pleased to supply your requirements direct against a cheque or
VISA/ACCESS settlement and the £10 voucher. If you choose to pay by
cheque or credit card, please complete the attached card and return it to
us with your order.

Yours faithfully
HIE-LAND INDUSTRIES LIMITED

Philip S Bootson
MARKETING MANAGER

Encs 1)   "Guide to Central Heating" booklet with £10 voucher
      2)   Hugotrol 90/95M data sheet
      3)   List of distributors
      4)   Card for cheque/VISA/ACCESS settlement

Key to Assignments 67 and 68

HIE-LAND INDUSTRIES LIMITED

Hie-Land House
77 Cassel Park Lane
Bridgeside
EDINBURGH
EH2 4AF

Telex 939203

VAT Reg No 414 7677 37

Telephone 031-557 4571

Our ref BJD/SDW/your initials

(Today's date)

Miss Kirsty Darwen
49 South Crumsden Road
Glasnevin
EDINBURGH
EH7 4MX

Dear Miss Darwen

CHANGE OF APPOINTMENT

I confirm the following changes in your employment, as discussed at our annual staff review interview on (last Tuesday's date).

New post	Technical Support Manager
Branch	Darlington
Department	Technical Services
New salary	£14,395
Car user grade	VI

These changes are effective from (1st of next month's date). I enclose a copy of the revised Conditions of Service for this post.

May I take this opportunity of thanking you for your efforts during the past year, and wish you every success in your new appointment.

Yours faithfully
HIE-LAND INDUSTRIES LIMITED

BRIDGET J DANVERS
Chief Personnel Manager

Enc

Key to Assignment 69

HIE-LAND INDUSTRIES LIMITED

Hie-Land House
77 Cassel Park Lane
Bridgeside
EDINBURGH
EH2 4AF

Telex 939203

VAT Reg No 414 7677 37

Telephone 031-557 4571

Our ref BJD/CDA/your initials

(Today's date)

Miss R A Pringle
52a Brook Buildings
Baxter Street
SCARBOROUGH
North Yorkshire
YO11 3VK

Dear Miss Pringle

PROFESSIONAL WORK PLACEMENT

As agreed with your tutors, we shall be happy to accept you at Hie-Land
House for your six-month Professional Work Placement period.

I enclose a brochure, which gives an outline of the company's history and
development. As you are probably aware, we are currently celebrating the
Centenary of the founding of the company. The brochure also gives
details of the many and varied products we manufacture and sell, and I
hope this will be of use in the preparation of your background notes for
your thesis.

I have now worked out a provisional programme for you, and have tried as
far as possible to relate this to the main areas of interest in your
degree course. An outline of the programme is given below, and a
detailed schedule will be given to you on arrival.

MONTH ONE

The first two weeks will be spent in the Publicity and Public Relations
Department. This will help you to gain some background to the workings
of the company before you move into the other departments. The second
two weeks will be spent in the Advertising Department.

MONTH TWO

Your second month will be spent in the Accounts Department, gaining an
insight into the computerised accounting system used by the company.

2
(Today's date)
Miss R A Pringle

MONTH THREE

Although production control is not specifically mentioned in your tutor's
request, we feel that you would benefit from a month spent in our
Production Control Department, which has a central co-ordinating function
in the company.

MONTH FOUR

Your period with the Central Training Department will involve you in a
variety of ways. You will be given experience of the organisation and
operation of the Central Training Department, and may perhaps be called
upon to act as an instructor/lecturer for some of our courses for office
staff. Towards the end of the month you will take part, as a trainee, in
the Sales Courses, as a preparation for your period spent in the Sales
Department.

MONTH FIVE In your fifth month you will spend two weeks in the Central
Purchasing Department, and the rest of the month in the Sales Department.

MONTH SIX You will spend one week with me in the Central Personnel
Department, before returning to the Accounts Department, where you will
be able to take a more informed interest in the operation and functions
of this department in the light of your experience throughout the
previous five months.

I think this programme will give you a varied and valuable insight into
the operation of a large organisation. If there are any changes you
would like to make, please let me know as soon as possible, and I shall
do my best to incorporate your ideas.

My secretary, Miss Vince, will be writing to you within the next week or
so with details of arrangements for your accommodation while you are in
Edinburgh. We look forward to meeting you.

Yours sincerely
HIE-LAND INDUSTRIES LIMITED

Bridget J Danvers
Chief Personnel Manager

Enc

Key to Assignment 70

HIE-LAND INDUSTRIES LIMITED

Hie-Land House
77 Cassel Park Lane
Bridgeside
EDINBURGH
EH2 4AF

Telex 939203

VAT Reg No 414 767 737

Telephone 031-557 4571

Our ref   BGO/IPG42/SK/your initials

Your ref   LRGG/SY

(Today's date)

Dear Mr Goodison

INFORMATION SYSTEMS MEETING

As arranged, I enclose a copy of the notice we have circulated to our members – and other interested people – about the meeting on Thursday, 27 January.

I confirm that we are satisfied, for the purposes of the demonstration, if you connect two of your facsimile machines. Mr Torres, of our Technical Support Department, will be present, and will give you any assistance you need.

We expect your demonstration to take place between 6.45 pm and 7.45 pm. If you would like to hear Colin Tinsdale's talk at 5.30 pm, we should be happy for you to arrive early enough to set up your equipment before he begins. Please let me know what time you expect to arrive.

We will not know exactly how many people will be attending until nearer the date, but expect it to be around 35–40 people.

Yours sincerely

Basil Ormerod
Secretary
Staff Information Systems Club

Mr L R G Goodison
Travos (UK) PLC
Travos House
77 Bruce Avenue
EDINBURGH
EH2 4WD
Enc

Key to Assignment 71

ALLEGRA COTTAGE   RUSSELL AVENUE   FALKIRK   FK4 7QQ

TELEPHONE 0324-776478

(Today's date)

Dear Miss Carnegie

I saw your advertisement in the local newspaper about your research into your family connections with Falkirk.

As I have made a hobby of tracing my family history, I have gathered together quite a collection of information about the Carnegie family/ies in Falkirk. There is every likelihood that details of your ancestors are recorded in the material I have amassed.

If you will send me further information to supplement the brief details in your advertisement, I shall be happy to try to trace relevant references in my notes. I look forward to hearing from you.

Yours sincerely

Alexander Firth-Carnegie

Miss Johanna Carnegie
1774 South Lake Drive
PEORIA
Illinois 61622
USA

The spelling errors were: conections (connections); traceing (tracing); quiet (quite); Their (There); likelyhood (likelihood); suppliment (supplement); relavant (relevant); forword (forward); sinserely (sincerely).

Key to Assignment 72

```
HIE–LAND INDUSTRIES LIMITED            Telex 939203
Hie-Land House   77 Cassel Park Lane
Bridgeside  EDINBURGH  EH2 4AF         Tel 031-557 4571
```

Da(te a)s Postmark

Thank you for your application t(oo) attend our (Centen-)
Centenary Celebration Open Day. (we) (a)pologise for this
formal metho(do)f acknowledging your application, but
(but) we have received (a) unexpectedly large (no) of
applications. Your official invitatio(n &) further
details will be sent to you within a few (a few days)

```
HIE–LAND INDUSTRIES LIMITED            Telex 939203
Hie-Land House   77 Cassel Park Lane
Bridgeside  EDINBURGH  EH2 4AF         Tel 031-557 4571


Date as Postmark

Thank you for your application to attend our Centenary
Celebration Open Day.  We apologise for this formal
method of acknowledging your application, but we have
received an unexpectedly large number of applications.
Your official invitation and further details will be
sent to you within a few days.
```

Did you remember to address the reverse side of the card to Mr Forster?

Key to Assignment 73

a. File.

b. The date, the addressee or inside address, the salutation, the body of the letter and the complimentary close.

c. The page number, the date, and the name of the addressee.

d. A form letter or a skeleton letter.

e. The date, the addressee's name and address, the salutation, and the complimentary close.

Key to Assignment 74

<u>HAIR CREATIONS INTERNATIONAL - DARVILLE</u>

<u>Open Monday to Saturday - Late Night Thursday</u>

	<u>Junior Designer</u>	<u>Designer</u>	<u>Advanced Designer</u>	<u>Stylist</u>	<u>Tutor</u>
Cut and Blow	£2.95	£3.85	£4.65	£7.00	£8.25
Perms from	£6.10	£7.65	£8.95	£16.00	£17.50
Highlights	£4.75	£4.75	£5.60	£11.00	£16.70

Key to Assignment 75

DELLAMERE SURGERY STOOL

The comfortable Dellamere Surgery Stool has been ergo-nomically designed for correct posture and incorporates a fully-adjustable backrest. The new gas-lift height adjustment is guaranteed for 2 years. Safety features include a chrome-plated 5-star base with a foot ring. The attractive upholstery is fully flame-retardant and hard-wearing.*

MODEL NUMBER	MODEL	STYLE	PRICE**
DSS/202	Cherie	Without backrest	£96.00
DSS/200	Caroline	With backrest	£109.00
KSS/001	Camilla	De luxe model	£165.00

*   Colours available: black, grey, tan, champagne and blue

**   Prices shown exclude VAT

Key to Assignment 76

WYNNSFORD MOTOR COMPANY LIMITED

WYNNSFORD GARAGE

Opening Hours	From	To
	HOURS	HOURS
PETROL		
Monday to Saturday	0730	2200
Sunday and Bank Holidays	0900	1700
REPAIRS AND BODY SHOP		
Monday to Friday	0830	1700
Saturday	0900	1400
SALES AND HIRE		
Monday to Friday (Summer)	0830	2000
Monday to Friday (Winter)	0830	1900
Saturday	0900	1730
Sunday	1030	1700
PARTS DEPARTMENT		
Monday to Friday	0830	1730
Saturday	0900	1400

Key to Assignment 77

S T O C K L I S T

STOCK SIZES	KG PER 1,000 SHEETS		
	60 g/m^2	70 g/m^2	85 g/m^2
SRA2 (45 cm x 64 cm)	17.3 kg	20.2 kg	24.5 kg
RA2 (43 cm x 61 cm)	--	18.4 kg	22.3 kg
Double Cap (43 cm x 69 cm)	17.8 kg	20.8 kg	25.2 kg
Large Post (42 cm x 53 cm)	13.4 kg	15.6 kg	18.9 kg

Key to Assignment 78

HIE-LAND INDUSTRIES LIMITED

Hie-Land House
77 Cassel Park Lane
Bridgeside
EDINBURGH
EH2 4AF

Telex 939203

VAT Reg No 414 7677 37

Telephone 031-557 4571

Our ref HT/your initials

(Today's date)

Dear Customer

Thank you for your enquiry about WUNDAWHITE boards. Our new range of
white-boards offers a variety of surfaces and features. The patented
surfaces of WUNDAWHITE boards accept "wet-wipe" or "dry-wipe" markers and
double as projection screens. We give below a table which should help
you to select the most appropriate board for your purposes.

BOARD	WHAT IT WILL DO	WHAT IT WILL NOT DO	PRICE*
Magawhite 6' x 4'	Dry wipe	Wet wipe Hold magnets	£110.50
Markawhite 6' x 4'	Wet wipe Hold magnets	Dry wipe	£126.75
Magnawhite 5' 4" x 4' (Double-sided)	Dry wipe Hold magnets	Wet wipe Give low-glare projection	£115.50
Writewhite 6' x 4'	Wet/dry wipe Hold magnets	Give low-glare projection	£102.75

*   Prices exclude VAT

All WUNDAWHITE boards are designed and made in the United Kingdom to the
highest standards. WUNDAWHITE boards are extremely light in relation to
their size, which makes them easy to handle and truly portable.

We enclose a copy of our latest catalogue and price list and look forward
to receiving your order.

Yours sincerely

HOWARD THINGWALL

Sales Manager

Enc

Key to Assignment 79

COSTA BLANCA FOR A WINTER HOLIDAY

Average Temperatures and Hours of Sunshine

	OCT	NOV	DEC	JAN	FEB	MAR	APR
	TEMPERATURE						
Average maximum daytime temperature	76 °F	68 °F	62 °F	60 °F	63 °F	67 °F	70 °F
	HOURS OF SUNSHINE						
Average maximum hours of sunshine	6.7	6.0	5.6	5.8	6.8	7.1	8.7

Key to Assignment 80

C H A R M I A N   L I N E S

Passenger Fares

Single Fare Per Person (Excluding Meals)	Low Season		High Season	
	Weekdays Mon–Fri	Weekends Sat–Sun	Weekdays Mon–Fri	Weekends Sat–Sun
Sleeperette	£55	£65	£95	£105
4–Berth Cabin	£85	£95	£115	£125
2–Berth Cabin	£97	£107	£127	£137
De–Luxe Cabin	£127	£137	£155	£165
Stateroom	£142	£152	£166	£176

Children under 4 years free provided no extra berth required.

Key to Assignment 81

M E M O R A N D U M

FROM   Mr K G Knight   REF   KGK/your initials

TO   Miss B W Wroxford   DATE   (Today's date)

CONFERENCE FACILITIES - TREVALLAN HOTEL

As requested, I called in at the Trevallan Hotel when I visited
the Norwich Offices last week and the Conference Manager kindly
gave me a guided tour of the conference facilities. The hotel has
5 suitable rooms - details as below.

Room/Suite	Seating Capacity		
	Theatre Style	Banquet	Exhibition Square Metres
Alvardo Hall ..	150	150	186
Salmeda	75	50	93
Wareham	85	50	90
Lady Villeneuve	60	40	82
Fermor	45	45	54
Norvena	30	12	42

Although we originally thought of using one large hall, I feel -
after viewing the rooms - that our best plan would be to hire the
Wareham and Lady Villeneuve suites. These 2 rooms have sliding
doors between them, and this would give us some flexibility in
layout of the conference room and the exhibition materials.

I enclose a leaflet giving floor plans and measurements of the
various rooms, which you should find useful. As soon as I know
whether you agree with my suggestion I will let you have some
provisional costings.

Enc

The spelling errors were: conferance (conference); Meters (Metres); originaly (originally); flexability
(flexibility); wether (whether); provissional (provisional).

Key to Assignment 82

MODEL	LENGHT	TYPE	NUMBER OF BERTHS	FEATURES	PRICE*
Woodland Fern	22' 0"	Static Van	5 Berths	No Shower	£4,999
Moorland Heather ...	24'	Static Van	5 Berths	Shower	£5,245
Fenland Reed	25' 9"	Static Van	6 Births	Shower	5,499
Upland Rose.	27'9"	Static Van	8 Berths	Shower	£5,750
Highland Heatherbell	30' 0"	Static Van	9 berths	Shower	£6255
Lowland Gorse ....;	33' 9'	Static Van	10 Berth	No Show r	£6,950

* Exclusing Vat

F L O R A   C A R A V A N S

MODEL	LENGTH	TYPE	NUMBER OF BERTHS	FEATURES	PRICE*
Woodland Fern	22' 0"	Static Van	5 Berths	No Shower	£4,999
Moorland Heather ...	24' 0"	Static Van	5 Berths	Shower	£5,245
Fenland Reed	25' 9"	Static Van	6 Berths	Shower	£5,499
Upland Rose	27' 9"	Static Van	8 Berths	Shower	£5,750
Highland Heatherbell	30' 0"	Static Van	9 Berths	Shower	£6,255
Lowland Gorse	33' 9"	Static Van	10 Berths	No Shower	£6,950

*   Excluding VAT

INDEX

Assignments involving specific skills are listed in italics.

HIE-LAND INDUSTRIES LIMITED

Hie-Land House
77 Cassel Park Lane
Bridgeside
EDINBURGH
EH2 4AF

Telex 939203

VAT Reg No 414 7677 37

Telephone 031-557 4571

M E M O R A N D U M

FROM   REF

TO   DATE